Pets By Royal Appointment

BRIAN HOEY

THE AUTHOR OF THE BESTSELLING
Not in Front of the Corgis

Pets By Royal Appointment

SECRETS OF THE ROYAL FAMILY AND THEIR ANIMALS

Biteback Publishing

This paperback edition published in Great Britain in 2019 by
Biteback Publishing Ltd
Westminster Tower
3 Albert Embankment
London SE1 7SP
Copyright © Brian Hoey 2013, 2019

ISBN 978-1-78590-510-0

Contents

Acknowledgements

I have been very fortunate when preparing this book to be able to call on the help and cooperation of many people who have been unstinting with their time and patience.

It was inevitable that I would need accurate information from the royal household and I am glad to be able to record my appreciation to, among others, David Pogson in the Buckingham Palace press office for supplying the names of all the horses the Queen (and as Princess Elizabeth) has ridden at the Sovereign's Birthday Parade (Trooping the Colour); David Rankin-Hunt and Sophie Hetreed in the Royal Collection at St James's Palace for their help with factual matters concerning archive material; and the former press secretary to the Prince of Wales, Paddy Harveson, and his colleague, Amanda Foster, at Clarence House for all the details of the pets belonging to His Royal Highness, the Duchess of Cornwall, the Duke and Duchess of Cambridge and Prince Harry.

Colin Sealy at the Kennel Club provided invaluable information regarding the various pedigrees of royal dogs – corgis, cocker spaniels and Labradors – while Cindy Lass told me about her experience at Buckingham Palace of painting the royal corgis. My thanks also go to Lady Pamela Hicks for her contribution.

Gordon Wise and Richard Pike at my agents Curtis Brown have handled the mind-boggling intricacies of contracts and delivery dates, while publisher Jeremy Robson is the man who was responsible for the idea of the book in the first place and, with his team, including managing editor Hollie Teague and designer Namkwan Cho, has seen it through to its conclusion. And my special thanks to Olivia Beattie of Biteback Publishing for this new paperback edition.

Thank you everyone. And of course, my respectful gratitude must go to Her Majesty and her family, for providing the basis on which this entire project is based.

As usual, all opinions, unless otherwise stated, are mine and mine alone – as are any and all errors!

Brian Hoey

Prologue

The royals say they can do without many things, but not their animals. They are suspicious of practically everyone outside their own family and the only creatures they really trust are not of the human variety.

Royalty has always realised that the sycophancy practised by courtiers for centuries is totally false and is in no way personal. It goes with the job. That is why they have become cynical and suspicious of all but their canine and feline friends. Their pets have no knowledge of the status or rank of their owners, neither do they care; they are the most loyal of companions, not looking for advancement nor hoping for preference. All they want is to be loved and looked after.

A canine companion has accompanied every sovereign since Henry VIII (1509–47) and probably many before him, though his father Henry VII (1485–1509) so hated dogs that he had them banned from court.

For countless monarchs and their consorts, cats, dogs, horses and even the occasional parrot have acted as constant, faithful companions, unquestioning allies and surrogate children. Generations of isolated royal children have discovered their main sources of comfort and warmth were often their pet dogs and cats. In his memoirs, the Duke of Windsor emphasised this point when he wrote that 'Kings and Queens are only secondarily fathers and mothers', which is why he and his siblings lavished their affections almost exclusively on their pets. Today dogs, in particular, occupy a very special place in royal life. Not one member of the royal family, male or female, can imagine being without a canine companion.

Her Majesty's corgis, the most pampered but disliked creatures at court – by almost everyone except the Queen – even have their own 'mini palaces' immediately outside their mistress's sitting room in Buckingham Palace. The staff all know that they are totally unimportant compared to the Queen's animals. As they put it, 'We can be replaced tomorrow; the dogs cannot.'

As an integral part of her job, the Queen has been painted hundreds of times, the most recognisable portrait being the famous work by Pietro Annigoni. One day, when the artist felt the sitting had not gone too well, he kicked one of her corgis – out of her sight, of course – sending it sliding across the floor into a grandfather clock. The clock began working for the first time in years!

When Michael Fagan broke into Buckingham Palace in 1982 and the Queen woke to find him sitting on her bed bleeding from a cut to his hand, she later said he was lucky the corgis had not been in the room or they might have torn him to pieces. An exaggeration, perhaps, but they can be extremely ferocious little creatures.

An elderly bishop visiting the Queen at Sandringham received a rude awakening when he sat in a comfortable chair and dozed for a few minutes. He put his feet up on what he thought was a convenient footstool only to have it suddenly come to life and give his ankle a nasty nip. It was, of course, one of Her Majesty's pets lying outstretched on the carpet. The Queen discreetly hid her laughter but she was plainly very amused at the incident.

In 2000, Elizabeth Taylor was made a Dame of the British Empire. She begged the Palace to allow her to bring her own dog along to her investiture, thinking the Queen would welcome another dog lover. But the household was adamant that no dogs could be permitted and she came alone.

Dogs have been favoured by the royal family because they have a natural instinct to remain unquestioningly loyal. When the Queen is working hard at her desk in Buckingham Palace, her corgis lie contentedly at her feet and she finds comfort in their silent presence. They neither ask for nor expect constant attention, just companionship. A dog will stay by the side of his master or mistress through thick or thin; some royal pet dogs have pined so much when their owner has died that they too have passed away shortly afterwards.

The Queen's corgis have an irritating habit of yapping – she calls it canine barking – at the most inconvenient times. However, Her Majesty has a pet cure to stop them making too much noise if she is on the telephone or entertaining guests. She carries a small supply of mixer biscuits in her pocket and surreptitiously feeds them. They are immediately silenced – at least that's the theory.

The Queen's grandmother Queen Mary did not, as a rule, care for dogs. But, during the Second World War when she moved to Badminton to avoid the bombing in London, she found a little dog that quickly became her pet. Just like her granddaughter, she too used to carry a handful of dog biscuits to feed it in the dining room after dinner every evening. On one occasion another guest, yet again an elderly bishop, was handed one of the biscuits and invited to feed the animal. His Grace was rather deaf and thought the biscuit was intended for him. He ate it, believing he was undergoing a strange royal initiation test.

The Queen Mother loved to relate a story about someone else's dog when she was on a private visit to Rhodesia (now Zimbabwe). At a dinner given in her honour by the acting governor general in Salisbury (now Harare), she was involved in a slightly embarrassing incident – not that it bothered her, only the other guests. Her host owned a huge pet dog named Timmy, a giant cross-bred Great Dane and Airedale terrier that weighed over ten stone. Timmy went everywhere with his master and during the banquet lay quietly under the table. When it became time for the ladies to withdraw, they all got up, except the Queen Mother, who explained sweetly, 'I'm terribly sorry, but I cannot leave the table. Timmy Tredgold (named after the governor, his master) is sitting on my dress.' She told the story many times when she returned to Britain.

One rarely hears about any of the Queen's other animals, apart from her horses of course, but she is also one of the world's most successful owners and breeders of racing pigeons with a luxurious loft based at Sandringham. This is also where she keeps her kennels of famous – and very valuable – black and yellow Labradors, which are sold around the world for thousands of pounds. All buyers are carefully vetted before they are approved.

Each member of the royal family has a pet preference and each makes sure his or her favourite is given every creature comfort. As well as their mini palaces, the Queen's corgis have expensive tailored Burberry raincoats to protect them from the wet; Her Majesty's gun dogs at Sandringham have 'houses' with a lawn in front so they can stretch their legs; Princess Anne allows her dogs to ride alongside her in her Bentley without any need for covering on the immaculate leather seats; the Duchess of Cornwall's Jack Russells are given the run of all her homes, with no rooms out of bounds, and are allowed to sit wherever they like, even on the silk-upholstered chairs.

Prince Charles is regarded as the most demanding of royal employers. His temper tantrums are legendary and he is even feared on occasion by his siblings and cousins, all of whom have, at some time or other, felt his anger and the sharp edge of his tongue. But they all agree that not once has he ever been heard to speak harshly to one of his animals; the idea of hitting or kicking them simply would not occur to him. In fact, he dotes on them all.

The royals all know that the loyalty they receive from their pets cannot be repeated on a human level – and neither would they want it to be. Even today, the Queen often chats to her corgis, and her footmen and maids all understand they are not to interfere when these one-way conversations are taking place.

It is hard to believe, but the Queen is already well into the second half of her ninth decade – and still going strong. She has quite obviously inherited the longevity genes of her mother and so too have some of her pets. Several of the corgis have reached her age in dog years and both appear to thrive on their mutual affection and companionship. Her Majesty says much of the credit for her well-being must go to her animals and the way they have kept her young at heart.

The conceit of royal pets is something members of the royal household have quickly learned to accept. They do not obey anyone except their royal owners and the aura of royalty appears to have rubbed off on most of them.

The late Countess Mountbatten of Burma (Prince Philip's cousin) summed up beautifully the relationship between royalty and their pets when she recalled King George V's sentiment: 'Only an emperor and a dog can walk through a doorway without looking to see if anyone else is there. They share a lofty arrogance.'

1

Princesses and their Pets

The Queen's passion for animals has developed into a lifelong love affair that shows no sign of diminishing in the latter years of her life. It began in 1928 when she was just two years old. Her father, then Duke of York and later King George VI, moved the family (there were only three of them then; Princess Margaret wasn't born until 1930) out of London to Naseby Hall in Northamptonshire for the hunting season. It was the sort of thing that royalty and the aristocracy did in those far off days. It was there that the infant Elizabeth was introduced to horses and hounds for the first time and she found, even at that tender age, that she was not intimidated by the animals. She loved to pat them and, because she showed no fear, she had to be restrained by her nursemaid from getting too close on occasions. She didn't realise that horses and hounds could bite.

Princesses Elizabeth and Margaret grew up surrounded

by animals. When they lived at 145 Piccadilly in London (today the site of a five-star hotel without even a plaque on the wall to mark who once lived there), where the family had moved in 1927, and where the young princesses would spend the next ten years before moving across the road to Buckingham Palace, their father felt it was important for them not only to own dogs but to understand the responsibility required to take care of them.

The duke, known to the family as Bertie, bought his first Pembroke corgi in 1933 from the respected Rozavel kennels in Surrey. The breed was relatively unknown in those days, but the duke and duchess were not put off by the initial lack of a lengthy pedigree.

A lady named Mrs Thelma Gray, who was a well-known breeder, was asked to bring a selection of puppies from the kennels to 145 Piccadilly. Elizabeth and Margaret wanted to keep them all but eventually they chose a little corgi with the official name of Rozavel Golden Eagle, simply because he was the only one with even a stump of a tail. The princesses didn't realise that corgis are not intended to sport a tail. Renamed Dookie (the name was a contraction of Duke of York and was first used by servants and then finally adopted by the

Yorks when they realised the dog would only respond to that name), the dog hated everyone except Elizabeth and Margaret and he was prone to biting anyone but the two girls.

On one occasion a very senior politician was visiting the duke and duchess when he allowed his hand to dangle over the side of his chair. Immediately Dookie seized the offending hand and refused to let go, drawing blood. The princesses didn't blame the dog, saying it was his natural instinct and the injured man must have provoked him, proving that, even as children, they believed that their dogs were blameless. They would continue with this belief throughout their lives.

On another occasion, a visitor, Lord Lothian, attempted to pat Dookie on the head only to have a chunk bitten out of his hand. There was blood all over the floor and the poor man needed medical attention. 'Oh dear,' was the children's mother's only remark and Dookie was not even reprimanded.

In those early days when Dookie was the pride and joy of the York household, a member of staff was instructed to take the corgi to the veterinary surgery as the canine had been unwell. The footman had good reason not to welcome the order as he, like most of the rest of the staff, had been snapped at in the past.

On arrival at the vet's office the footman offered to lift

Dookie on to the examination table only to be informed, in a supercilious tone, that no assistance was required: 'I have had some experience with dogs.' The footman stood clear as the vet attempted to lift Dookie and was promptly bitten on the hand. If the royal servant had a little self-satisfied smirk on his face, and who could blame him, he managed to conceal it from the injured vet.

Along with Dookie came Jane (Lady Jane), with whom Dookie would soon be mated. Jane gave birth to two puppies on Christmas Eve, which naturally caused the seven-year-old Princess Elizabeth to name them Carol and Crackers. Carol was the runt of the small litter and was put to sleep shortly after her birth, but Crackers lived to be twenty years old.

Both Dookie and Jane became deeply attached to their young mistresses. The only way to tell the two corgis apart was that Jane's face was a slightly darker shade of brown.

When the Yorks moved at weekends from central London to Royal Lodge, their magnificent country home in Windsor Great Park (given to them by King George V in 1931) the dogs were waiting for them when they arrived. The girls particularly enjoyed playing with them in the little thatched cottage Y Bwthyn Bach, a gift from the people of Wales to Princess Elizabeth on her 6th birthday. As the princesses went about their everyday chores, washing and cleaning the house, never leaving any mess for servants to clear up after them, the dogs would scamper in every room upstairs and down.

It was said that Dookie was the outstanding 'character' of the canine family who tried, not always successfully, to impose his will on the rest. He was also the only one who fought the other dogs, avoiding the yellow Labradors because of their size.

Dookie always insisted on sitting closest to Princess Elizabeth and any of the other dogs who tried to take his place were quickly made aware of their correct position in the order of things. Indeed, throughout her adult life one of the Queen's corgis has always established itself as the boss.

Because of their size, the girls were able to take Dookie and Jane with them when they visited friends and relations' houses – though they were not always welcomed if the hosts had pets of their own.

Dookie died of natural causes in 1940 and Jane was killed in a car accident in Windsor Great Park in 1944 after being run over by one of the estate workers. The man was devastated but Princess Elizabeth wrote him a personal note to reassure him that he was not to blame.

As well as the corgis, the girls loved the three yellow Labradors, Mimsy, the Duke of York's favourite, and her son and daughter Stiffy and Scrummy, who, although very much the property of their father, were an integral part of the York family. In spite of their size, the gentle nature of Labradors meant they would tolerate the antics of the smaller dogs – including Dookie! – when they leapt up and tried to get them to play. Indeed, so affectionate were the Labradors that when Princess Elizabeth introduced Jane to Mimsy in the little Welsh cottage, the two played contentedly together.

Judy was a golden retriever who spent hours in the company of Ben, a black cocker spaniel, a favourite of the duchess. Another member of the group, Choo-Choo, a shih tzu, preferred his own company and rarely mixed with the others. Choo-Choo was the scruffiest looking of all the royal dogs with his woolly coat and perhaps that is why he became a favourite, certainly of

Princess Margaret. He was so named by the Duchess of York because when he first arrived at their home he made them all laugh as he tried to hurry across the lawn puffing and blowing like a steam engine.

In the York household there was only one master, the duke himself, and when all the dogs were playing with the duchess and the girls in the garden, he only had to make an appearance for them all to be forgotten as the dogs rushed to be the first to be fondled by the duke. No matter how close the princesses were to their little corgis, or the duchess to her cocker spaniel, the dogs all knew who their real master was, and he was delighted. He seemed to inspire in his dogs a devotion far beyond that normally associated with animals and their owners. And the feeling was mutual.

The Duke of York was arguably the most loving father of any generation in the royal family and, although he had public duties to perform as the second son of King George V, he was first and foremost a family man, husband and father, who never expected that within a few short years he would be called upon to accept the awesome responsibilities of becoming king and emperor. As such he was able to indulge his children and their pets in a manner no other person in his position had been allowed to do before.

He had a wonderful philosophy regarding his animals,

which he passed on to his daughters. It was not enough just to own a dog, but one also had to love them. He said if you made your dog happy, it would return your affection and also prove to be the most loyal of friends throughout its lifetime. The princesses would in turn pass these lessons onto their own children.

The princesses' dogs enjoyed a luxurious existence. The 1930s was a time of depression in most of Great Britain, but in royal homes there was no shortage and the dogs benefited accordingly. While the princesses lavished love in abundance on their pets they, in turn, received enormous benefits themselves by learning how to handle and care for their animals personally. The duke and duchess made sure their daughters looked after the dogs and didn't expect servants to clean up after them.

The princesses' love of animals was not confined to their domestic pets. They doted on all creatures, large and small, wild or timid.

On one occasion mice were detected at 145 Piccadilly, as they were in practically every other house in the land at that time. In upper- and middle-class homes it was the custom to call in the 'Vermin Man', who specialised in exterminating mice and rats and any other kind of rodent.

When Elizabeth and Margaret were told that one of the ways in which mice were destroyed was by baiting a trap with treacle so the mouse would become stuck and eventually starve to death, they were horrified and persuaded their father to order the 'Vermin Man' not to use this cruel method but to find some other more humane way of ridding the house of mice. Even then, their father had to insist that they did not 'rescue' the offending mouse and give him a good home in their bedroom, which is what they wanted to do.

Elizabeth had thirty miniature toy horses, each one a foot high, with a saddle and bridle that had to be carefully removed every night before she went to bed. She knew the names of every one and which one lived in which little 'stable' in the house. She kept those miniatures until the day she married in 1947 and no doubt they are still stored somewhere in one of the royal cupboards (royalty rarely discards anything). She loved horses from the moment she could ride and she told her governess, Marion (Crawfie) Crawford, that 'if ever I am queen, I shall make a law that there must be no riding on Sundays. Horses should have a rest, too. And I shan't let anybody dock their pony's tail.' Her first riding instructor was Mr Owen, who had been her father's groom at Naseby Hall. Mr Owen was a stern taskmaster but in later life Elizabeth said he taught her lessons she would never forget.

Her passion for horses extended to her reading matter, with *Black Beauty* among her early favourites, and the only clothes she was interested in, even when growing up, were her riding outfits. Each one was tailor made for her and she took endless pains to make sure she looked the part whenever she rode with her father in Windsor Great Park.

It has been well documented that the Queen has loved animals all her life. Dogs and horses have figured largely and at no period has she ever been without a pet. Even in the dark days of the Second World War, Elizabeth and her sister Margaret insisted on feeding their dogs themselves.

In 1944 when the court was at Windsor, Princess Alexandra, the daughter of the King of Greece, was a guest and she could not believe her eyes when she saw her cousins (Princesses Elizabeth and Margaret) feeding their dogs.

At tea time, and after receiving a nod from their mother, Princess Elizabeth and her sister Margaret entered the room with a footman, who was carrying four little bowls. The girls placed the bowls expertly near to the low tea table.

> Then with much concentration the little girls [Elizabeth was eighteen at the time] prepared a meal in each of the bowls. 'Ready,' Margaret sang out and Elizabeth, giving a final inspection, nodded. Two more small dogs answered their call. Then there were four of them, each eating from his own bowl. Not until the dogs were feeding happily did the girls come to have their tea.

In 1941, a bomb fell on Hampton Court Palace causing extensive damage in the mews and injuring one of the carriage horses that had, ironically, been evacuated from Buckingham Palace to escape the bombing.

The animal was taken to Windsor where the royal veterinary surgeon operated to remove shrapnel that had become embedded in his side revealing large gashes. Elizabeth was taken to the stables to see him and she was very concerned, worrying that he would not be able to lie down to sleep because of his wounds. She visited him every day for weeks until she was convinced that all was well and the horse was going to survive. It did, and actually returned to duty some time later.

The two princesses were not only sisters but the best of friends and they remained so until Margaret's death in February 2002. They were totally different in character: Elizabeth quiet and reserved; Margaret outgoing and flamboyant. But they shared a deep love of their pets, both in childhood and as adults. And it was this affection for all animals that had been instilled in them by their parents that they, in turn, passed on to their own children and grandchildren. Charles, Anne, Andrew and Edward are all animal lovers, as are Peter and Zara Phillips, Princes William and Harry, Princesses Beatrice and Eugenie, and Louise and Jamie, the children of the Earl and Countess of Wessex. So too are Princess Margaret's children, Viscount [David] Linley and his sister, Lady Sarah Chatto, and her grandchildren. And now the great-grandchildren of the Queen and Prince Philip are being introduced to country life and are learning to share the affection and respect for animals the family has always shown.

2

Family Favourites

The Queen has been associated with corgis – and later gun dogs – for most of her life. Before Dookie, her first pet dog was in fact a small cairn terrier that was given to her when she was three years old by her Uncle David, the Prince of Wales (later King Edward VIII and later still, Duke of Windsor), who doted on his niece.

When the York family lived at 145 Piccadilly the young Princess Elizabeth played all day with the family pets, the dogs that were always around and also the caged budgerigars that were not allowed the freedom of the house, unlike the pet parrot belonging to her grandfather King George V, across the road at Buckingham Palace, which was encouraged to go wherever it liked, with no rooms sacrosanct.

Shih tzus were favoured at court by many British monarchs including George VI, who owned the afore-mentioned Choo-Choo. But when Elizabeth II came to the throne she did not continue the custom of keeping the breed, possibly because of their unsavoury habit of eating their own faeces and the competition they might pose to her own clear favourites, the corgis.

During the Second World War, when the Blitz was at its most severe in London, the King's wife, Queen Elizabeth (as she had by then become), had Choo-Choo evacuated to her former family home at St Paul's Walden in Suffolk, which had been turned into a convalescent home. So the family lived in the lodge for the duration of the war. By this time the dog was getting on a bit and his temper was not of the best. But the country seemed to suit him and when Queen Elizabeth managed to visit him he recognised her straight away. On one occasion she was due to have a photograph taken with some of the patients and staff. Choo-Choo had been sleeping when she arrived and she didn't disturb him. But suddenly he woke up, sniffed the air and knew straight away that she was there. He threw himself on her and they both wrestled to the ground as Her Majesty laughed out loud as she played with her old pet. I know it's difficult to imagine this august lady in such circumstances, but I am assured it is true. Anyway, it's such a good story, I want it to be true. Choo-Choo then settled down and was quiet throughout the hours she spent with him – until it was time for her to go and then he started playing up again. Choo-Choo eventually died during the war and was succeeded by his grandson, Ching, who also won the hearts of the King and Queen.

Although Her Majesty was born in London and has lived most of her life in the city, she still regards herself primarily as a countrywoman at heart, with her interests being those of others of her generation and class. She likes nothing more than riding alone (apart from the ever watchful presence of a police protection officer) or walking accompanied only by a couple of her dogs. In the country, the Queen does not care what the weather is like: rain, snow, sleet, hail, freezing cold or blowing a gale, she still enjoys a good brisk walk. And she passed on to her children and grandchildren a respect for the countryside and all things animal, equestrian and canine.

Love of animals, particularly horses and dogs, is accepted as the natural way of things among royalty. They regard anyone who does not share their devotion to all four-legged creatures as being not quite normal. The Queen finds it curious that her three sons, Charles,

Andrew and Edward, do not care for horse racing with the passion that consumes her, even if they do (reluctantly) attend Royal Ascot out of a sense of duty. And her guests at Windsor or Sandringham are soon made aware that horses and dogs are a natural part of the daily programme. Indeed, the *Racing Post* is required reading at the royal breakfast table, where conversation is discouraged.

Royal children often liked to have their pet dogs – of the smaller variety – on their beds at night for very practical reasons: they kept them warm on cold winter nights. Royalty have always avoided heating their homes too much; ask any guest who has frozen when staying at Balmoral, even in August. Chilly bedrooms were made more welcoming after the pet dogs had lain there for a couple of hours before bedtime.

Prince Charles is a 'softie' who loves all his animals to distraction. When he was four years old, he owned a bull named Supreme and was delighted when the animal was named supreme champion at the annual Bath and

West Show, though at his age he wasn't altogether sure what the prize meant.

He and his sister Anne were allowed to keep pets in their nursery and they loved their hamster Chi-Chi, pet rabbit Harvey, which was a bit smaller than the giant imaginary rabbit in the hit film of that name, and two South American lovebirds. These had been given to them by the children's grandmother and Charles had named them David and Annie, after Davy Crockett and Annie Oakley, neither of whom he had ever heard of, so one can only assume the names must have been suggested by Grannie. Anne later had a cocker spaniel called Florence and, much later, their younger brother Prince Andrew was rarely seen without his pet Labrador, Francis.

In April 1994, Charles offered a reward of £30 to whoever found his pet Jack Russell bitch, Pooh, who went missing for several days when the family was at Balmoral. He was deeply distressed when, in spite of repeated rescue attempts, it was impossible to find the animal and bring her out of the rabbit hole they suspected she had become trapped in. Pooh was five. His Royal Highness was left with just the one Jack Russell, Tigger, another bitch and a gift from Lady Salisbury. When Tigger died, she was buried in the Azalea Walk at Highgrove and she is depicted in a carved stone embedded in the wall above her grave.

There are no dogs that Prince Charles does not like, but he does have one aversion to domestic animals: cats. Princess Margaret once gave him a kitten as a present when he was a child and he disliked it on sight. Since then, he has developed an aversion to everything feline and says he cannot even stand having one in the same room. He is said to be able to detect the presence of a cat when he enters a house even if the animal isn't there at the time. He was invited to stay at the home of friends in Scotland and when he discovered they owned a cat, they had to remove all traces before he was comfortable. And if, by chance, a cat happens to rub up against him, as cats sometimes will when they want to be stroked, he cannot bear to touch – or be touched – by one. He could not be classed as suffering from ailurophobia or the fear of cats; it's simply an aversion.

The late Diana, Princess of Wales, was also brought up surrounded by animals and when William and Harry were small she encouraged them to learn to ride, even though she had not ridden since she was thrown from her horse Romany when she was ten and had been frightened of all horses ever since. Diana did shed a tear, however, when Prince Charles's horse Allibar died in 1981. The ponies the boys rode had both been passed down from other members of the royal family and in turn they then passed them on to their younger cousins.

Diana wasn't too keen on Jack Russell terriers, believing they were a little too lively for her, but she thought spaniels much more gentle and easier to handle. When she moved into Kensington Palace she had several sent for her inspection, but none was finally chosen, in spite of the fact that William and Harry begged her for puppies.

The Duchess of Cornwall is fond of all animals (even cats, in spite of her husband's lack of affection for all domestic feline creatures); in fact, some people say that was one of the reasons Charles was attracted to her. She is not frightened by any animal or reptile, as was made apparent during her – and Prince Charles's – visit to south-east Asia and Australia in November 2012 as part of the celebrations to mark the Queen's Diamond Jubilee. Camilla was photographed many times holding a variety of animals, and not all of them were completely tame or house trained. She even indicated that she would have liked to bring a koala back from Australia, but Prince Charles's household managed to 'persuade' her otherwise.

Her Royal Highness's own pets at home are two Jack Russell terrier bitches, Beth and Bluebell. Before Beth and Bluebell came to be owned by Camilla, she had a beautiful Jack Russell named Freddy, who lived to be twenty-one years old before dying in 2009. Freddy had fathered Tosca, who in turn fathered Rosie; both died in 2011.

On the lookout for replacements for her Jack Russells, the duchess paid visits to Battersea Dogs and Cats Home. Rescued in August 2011 at just three months old, Beth, tri-colour with a tan-and-black-face and a black-and-white body, was described as a charming, confident little puppy. The chief executive officer was delighted that the duchess adopted the little dog: 'We know she will be very happy in her new home.'

In September 2012, the duchess visited Battersea once more and rescued nine-week-old Bluebell. Claire Horton, the head of Battersea, said:

> Once again the Duchess of Cornwall has given a second chance in life to a Battersea dog in need. Bluebell arrived … having had such an awful start in life, so we couldn't be happier that she caught the eye of the duchess and now has such a wonderful home … and will be an excellent companion for Beth.

The duchess insisted that she would pay the usual £105 'rehoming' charge that all adopters of rescue dogs are charged, even though the home's officials wanted to waive it in view of the favourable publicity they received by the duchess's gesture. The two little dogs are very much hers and hers alone. They know her voice and she loves to spend as much of her free time with them as she can.

Camilla is also an excellent horsewoman; some claim even better than her husband. She never loses an opportunity to ride whenever she can, though because of her public commitments, this is not as often as she would wish.

The Queen's third child, Prince Andrew, Duke of York, surprises some people when they learn that, contrary to their expectations, he does not own a Labrador or any other large dog, but the smallest of the working dogs. His Royal Highness is devoted to his two Norfolk terriers, which together with the Norwich terriers are moderately proportioned dogs, but too tough to be a toy breed. The staff at Sandringham have been heard to say that when Andrew leaves the house after Christmas, they would love him to forget to take his Norfolks with him; they are so fond of the dogs.

William and Kate, the Duke and Duchess of Cambridge, have a black English springer spaniel they have named Lupo. In 2012, they were given the puppy, born to a litter from Ella, the family dog of Kate's parents, Michael and Carole Middleton. Lupo starred in the first official pictures released by Kensington Palace of William and Kate with a baby Prince George, and he is obviously very special to all the family.

Harry and Meghan, the Duke and Duchess of Sussex, are both dog lovers too, and within months of their marriage in 2018 they welcomed a rescue beagle named Guy into their household, to be followed by a black Labrador puppy. There is plenty of room for both pets to run freely around in the couple's new home at Frogmore Cottage in the grounds of Windsor Castle.

The Queen Mother's favourite corgi, Crackers, was with her for many years and enjoyed a long and healthy life before dying in Coronation Year 1953 at the grand old age of fourteen. He had also enjoyed the affections of King George VI, who told several of his friends, 'He has the sweetest nature. He is never aggressive. The

Labradors must often try his patience, but he is always chummy and cheerful with them.' The only trouble with Crackers was that he did not like the opposite sex and adamantly refused to have anything to do with any of the bitches, so there were no sons or daughters.

When he became too old and decrepit to walk with her around the garden at Clarence House or Royal Lodge, she had a specially adapted bath chair built on which the dog would rest on a cushion while a footman pushed him around – much to the footman's barely concealed disgust. William Tallon, Her Majesty's long-serving page, used to delegate this unwanted task to one of the juniors; they always knew if they were out of favour if they drew this particular short straw.

The Queen Mother's love of animals, which in later life would be confined mainly, but not exclusively, to dogs and horses, included, when she was a child, her pet black Berkshire pig, upon which she doted. Unfortunately for her, her parents donated the animal as a raffle prize to a local garden fête. So Elizabeth and her brother David pooled their pocket money and even 'borrowed' some from the staff so they could buy all the raffle tickets. But, of course, it didn't work and someone else had the winning ticket. The future Queen Consort learned to cope with disappointment at an early age.

Her parents, realising how much the pig had meant

to her, made up for the loss by giving her a small pony called Bobs, to whom she immediately became very attached. Young children soon forget their woes.

Princess Margaret did not own corgis as an adult, as she knew they were the favourite breed of her sister (she was right) and she wanted something different. So she bought a Sealyham terrier called Johnny. However, within weeks of the dog's arrival at Kensington Palace the princess became ill and Johnny was dispatched to live with the Queen Mother at Royal Lodge. When Margaret was sufficiently recovered to take care of the dog once more, the Queen Mother said he seemed perfectly at home with her so why shouldn't he stay. Margaret agreed and her mother adopted Johnny.

The princess then acquired another Sealyham, which she called Pippin, and a Cavalier King Charles spaniel, named Rolly, therefore continuing the connection between royalty and the King Charles spaniels that had begun centuries before.

Princess Anne, though no one would describe her as someone who wears her heart on her sleeve, wept when one of her pet Labradors died. She was also distraught when Doublet, the mount that had carried her to equestrian supremacy in Europe, had to be painlessly put down. In this case, not only was the horse a valued companion but also an essential part of her sporting success. It was on Smith's Lawn at Windsor in 1974 that Doublet broke a leg and perhaps Anne was crying partly because of guilt on her part. Two veterinary surgeons had advised her that Doublet was not fit to ride on the day of the tragedy, but she overruled their objections and a broken leg was the result.

From childhood, the princess has attracted some notoriously bad-tempered canines – not that she would ever treat them unfavourably as a result. When one of her pit bull terriers savaged a favourite toy teddy bear she had cherished since she was an infant, the dog wasn't even chastised.

Instead, a conservator from the Royal Collection was summoned and ordered to restore the bear to its original, pristine condition. In fact, the bear could hardly have been described as 'pristine' before the attack after nearly sixty years' wear and tear. But the craftsman completed a perfect task and sent a bill for £300 to Anne.

She refused to pay what she thought was an exorbitant sum, so the Royal Collection eventually settled for £200, with the additional cost coming out of their budget. Royalty has always loved a bargain!

On one occasion another of the princess's pets, the

ferocious Dotty, almost ruined a dinner party that she and her husband, Timothy Laurence, were giving at their Gloucestershire home. For Anne, the matter didn't even warrant a reprimand, never mind a tear.

As the guests were sitting down to eat, an appalling stink pervaded the air. Nobody said a word. It was then discovered that Dotty had left a large 'deposit' on the carpet. The princess carried on as if nothing had happened, relating a long and complicated tale about a bird that allegedly escaped from a bear and then spoilt it all by boasting about its victory only to be overheard by the bear and eaten anyway. During this rambling anecdote a servant was summoned to clean up the mess and the dinner continued. One of the guests later revealed that although the dog mess was cleaned up, the appalling smell remained throughout the evening and was not conducive to a healthy appetite.

Dotty's bad behaviour only worsened. On Christmas Eve, when the princess arrived at Sandringham to join the rest of the family for the holiday, Dotty suddenly attacked Pharos, one of the Queen's elderly corgis, and savaged her to death.

Anne had rung the doorbell, with both her bull terriers, Dotty and Eglantyne, beside her, neither of whom was on a lead. Apparently, the noise of the bell excited the corgis – there were five with the Queen in her first-floor sitting room – and they ran downstairs. Rushing through the open door, Dotty clamped her powerful jaws on one of Pharos's hind legs, breaking it, and neither Anne nor a footman, who was also bitten, could prise them apart. The bull terrier shook the corgi 'like a doll', said a member of the household, and 'there was blood everywhere'. The Queen did not witness the attack; she was walking with the aid of a stick after an earlier knee operation and had to use the lift in the house (originally installed to help the Queen Mother, but she hated using it) to get down to the ground floor. Her Majesty was extremely distressed when she saw her pet in such agony and staff made an emergency call to Roger Harveson, the nearest vet, who has looked after the Sandringham animals for some years from his surgery in King's Lynn.

Mr Harveson sedated Pharos, but the animal was too far gone and too old to summon the strength to combat the attack and loss of blood. The next day the vet returned and, with the Queen's consent, quietly put Pharos down. It was the right thing to do; there was no chance of the corgi having any quality of life after such a ferocious attack.

But Her Majesty thought it impossible to blame Dotty as it was in the dog's make-up to attack other animals, so the bull terrier was not put down.

However, for Dotty, this was not a first offence. She

had bitten two boys in Windsor Great Park the previous year: one on the collarbone and leg and the other, a seven-year-old, on the back, arm and leg. The case went to court and Anne was fined £500 by East Berkshire magistrates after she pleaded guilty to letting her dog run out of control. She was also ordered to pay the children £500 and £148 in court costs. The children's parents were furious that the princess escaped with a small fine (the offence carried a possible £5,000 fine or six months' imprisonment, with the animal being destroyed). They said, 'We do not think justice has been done. The dog is still free and is a danger to society.' Anne's defence said that Dotty was a good-natured dog 'lacking in malice'. It was the evidence of Roger Mumford, the Queen's animal psychologist, that saved Dotty from being destroyed. Dr Mumford attends to the mental needs of the Queen's pets. He says that there is a pack mentality among any group of dogs and that this mentality can develop into a wariness of any newcomer.

At the hearing, Anne was also ordered to keep Dotty on a lead in public until she had attended appropriate obedience training. There is no record of Dotty – or Princess Anne – ever complying.

Dotty's mother, Florence, also had a bit of 'form': she bit a maid named Ruby Brooker, who was 'persuaded' not to take the matter any further.

Anne's daughter, Zara, known as Zara Phillips professionally but legally as Mrs Mike Tindall, has also ignored strict regulations with regard to her pet dogs. At the Burghley Horse Trials in 2009, she was 'walking' the course when she let her two dogs, Spey and Corley, loose to run and play. Spectators were appalled; although there were other animals around, Zara's were the only ones not on leads. But the officials did nothing to reprimand her.

The Duke of York's elder daughter, Princess Beatrice, is devoted to her Norfolk terrier, Max, who was given to her as a Christmas present when she was just thirteen years old. The dog is so cherished that in 2004 his face was emblazoned on a handbag costing £450 that Beatrice carried when she attended morning service at St George's Chapel, Windsor with the rest of the royal family at Easter that year. The following year Max's picture was used on the York family Christmas card.

Beatrice was understandably devastated when Max was attacked by some of the Queen's dogs during a walk at Balmoral. The terrier nearly lost an ear and his body was covered with horrific bites. He had to be seen by a vet immediately. Beatrice was not at Balmoral at the time – her father had taken Max up to Scotland for her – but she arrived shortly afterwards whereupon the Queen told her how upset she was that the incident had occurred. Roger Mumford was then called in to calm Her Majesty's animals – not poor old Max.

Max has been involved in a number of 'incidents' and on one occasion disappeared for three weeks from Royal Lodge (then Beatrice's home in Windsor Great Park) in 2008. Even the Queen joined in the search for the dog and they had all but given up hope when he suddenly walked alone back into the house, looking very sorry for himself with his left eye almost closed, bedraggled, soaking wet and obviously starving. Beatrice burst into tears when she saw him, but he was wagging his tail and after a bath and good meal he was soon his old self, lying in front of the fire with Beatrice scarcely able to believe her good luck. No one knew where he'd been but the theory was that perhaps he had chased a rabbit into its hole and become stuck. Max, it seems, is quite the survivor.

When quarantine was introduced in 1901, Edward VII took no notice of the regulations. In fact, no European monarch obeyed the law, believing that laws applied only to 'ordinary' people, never royalty.

During the Second World War, several European monarchs sought sanctuary in Britain and one, the former queen of Greece, attempted to smuggle her pet dachshund, Tulip, into the country when she was offered refuge. She did not declare the animal, fearing that the six months of quarantine would kill it off – and anyway, she said she couldn't bear to be without Tulip for that long. But during the disembarkation, the dog squealed and gave the game away. Customs officials ordered the small canine be taken to a dogs' home for the required period, but the former queen, who was heartbroken, was not prosecuted.

Her daughter, Queen Alexandra of Yugoslavia, commented that her mother 'had never been without a long-haired dachshund ... Now Tulip had been taken away and for quite an hour there was no consoling Mummie.'

In the present royal family, the Duke of Kent loves the company of his black Labrador, Frost, while his brother, Prince Michael of Kent, who is the current president of the Kennel Club, also owns a black Labrador, Shadow.

Though not a member of the royal family, Francis Egerton, the 8th Earl of Bridgewater, was one of the most eccentric of animal lovers.

He was known for giving the most elaborate dinner parties for dogs, where the animals were dressed in the finest fashions of the day, right down to fancy miniature shoes, all at enormous expense. Every night, up to a dozen dogs would be invited to dine at his table, each one served by its own servant while Egerton carried on conversations with the dogs about affairs of the day.

But this eccentricity paled into insignificance compared to the country actually ruled by a dog. In the year 1000 AD, Norway became the only country in the world to accept a dog as its ruler. An early king, Eystein, was hated by his people and overthrown. The people then chose a dog to rule, saying even it would be better than their previous king. The dog, named King Saur I, even had a state coronation and he 'reigned' for three years, signing laws with his paws before he was killed by a wolf and given a state funeral. True or false? Fact or just another shaggy dog story? Take your pick.

In the past, royalty (but not the British royal family) have gone to extreme and ridiculous length to preserve the exclusivity of their breeds, even arranging 'marriages' between their dogs with elaborate weddings costing thousands to stage and with sycophantic courtiers as 'guests' applauding the 'happy couple'.

Arguably the grandest wedding of them all took place in 1920 when the Nawab of Junagadh spent £22,000 on the nuptials of his favourite dog, Roshanara, and a golden retriever named Bobby.

The groom was accompanied by 250 dog 'attendants' dressed in jewelled brocade while a full military band played the wedding march. Bobby had gold bracelets on his paws, a gold necklace and a white silk cummerbund. His bride was carried on a solid silver palanquin to the Durbar Hall where the ceremony took place before a large congregation of Indian princes and other aristocrats. Only the British viceroy, Lord Irwin, declined his invitation.

After the marriage had been consummated, the bride retired to an air-conditioned room where she reclined on velvet cushions for the rest of her life while the Nawab attempted to anticipate her every wish.

Many parts of the United Kingdom are overrun by grey squirrels, with the red variety becoming rare. But there is a red squirrel community living and thriving in Scotland and the Queen is doing her best to preserve them on her estate at Balmoral. She has even erected signs stating that anyone walking or driving on her land should be aware of their presence: 'BEWARE SQUIRRELS CROSSING'.

She also regards the bats that haunt the upper reaches of the main hall at Balmoral Castle as (sort of) pets; well, they are a protected species, and Her Majesty refuses to allow any of her staff to disturb them, much to their secret amusement and occasional irritation when they have to clean up after them. When Her Majesty is in residence she spends part of every afternoon equipped with a butterfly net on an extended pole, catching the bats and then releasing them into the woods. Of course, being nocturnal creatures, they then return once night has fallen and she repeats the exercise the next afternoon. It's all harmless fun and gives her a sense of satisfaction that she is perhaps helping to preserve the species.

While cats are not generally favoured by most members of the royal family (including Prince Charles!), Princess

Michael of Kent loves the Burmese breed, an expensive and exclusive strain noted for its independent spirit and the fact that they insist on attaching themselves to only one person. They are definitely not pets for all the family, which is presumably why she likes them.

Shortly after Princess Elizabeth married Philip Mountbatten in 1947, she was sent a belated wedding present of a Siamese kitten, which she named Timmy. It was delivered to Buckingham Palace but the princess took it with her to her new home in the country where it remained until the couple moved to Clarence House.

For generations, royalty has cherished its pets, be they dogs, cats, birds, bears, rabbits, lizards, or even the more exotic creatures they have gathered from distant lands. Each animal has received affection and care from its royal owner in some cases far beyond that accorded to their own human families. And this mutual devotion can be traced back hundreds of years.

On 8 February 1587, when Mary, Queen of Scots was executed at Fotheringhay Castle, it is said that she secreted one of her pet Maltese dogs under her petti-coats as she was led to the execution block. The little dog was only discovered after the axe had fallen and he refused to leave the body of his mistress. He had to be dragged away and was saved from being destroyed when a friend of Mary, a French princess, took possession of him.

Not all animals have been favoured by monarchs, however. Some rulers have often expressed a fear or hatred of certain creatures and would not allow them anywhere near the court. In the reign of James I (1603–25) it was a well-known fact that His Majesty could not bear the sight (or sound) of pigs, so one night, a courtier, the Earl of Pembroke, secretly entered the royal bedchamber and deposited a huge pig in the bed. James was furious and terrified and vowed to get his own back. Discovering Pembroke's pet fear was frogs, he had several of his men hold the earl while frogs were placed inside his clothes.

Poodles are not a breed normally associated with royalty these days, but during the Civil War, when Charles I's forces fought with Oliver Cromwell's troops, Prince Rupert of the Rhine came to the aid of his Uncle

Charles and was accompanied everywhere by his white standard poodle, Boye. It was the first time a poodle had been seen in England and the Roundheads believed he possessed supernatural powers. However, as gallant and faithful as Boye was, he was just a normal, if rather large, dog and sadly he was killed at the Battle of Marston Moor in 1644.

And in the nineteenth century a poodle was a royal favourite at one of the minor Russian courts. Not only was he allowed to eat at the table with his master and mistress, but he was equipped with a pure linen napkin which was tied around his neck and a name plate, engraved in solid silver, indicated his position at the table.

His food, specially prepared in the royal kitchens (as it is for the Queen's corgis today), was served by a liveried footman who stood behind his chair, on which a cushion had been placed so that the animal was at the same height as everyone else. When he had finished eating, which he indicated by shaking his head from side to side, the servant would place his drinking bowl within easy reach. The dog also possessed a remarkable wardrobe of clothes, with each outfit a mirror of what his mistress was wearing on any particular day. Thankfully, the British royal family has never gone quite that far.

Winston Churchill was a great friend of five generations of royalty dating back to the Queen's great-grandfather, King Edward VII. In the early days of the Queen's reign, Churchill owned a pet poodle, Rufus, who was thoroughly spoilt. He used to have his dinner served on a plate that was placed on a cloth in the dining room where all the family and any guests were waiting for their evening meal. Nobody was allowed to start until Rufus had been served. On one occasion, after dinner the family settled down to watch the film *Oliver Twist*. As Bill Sikes tried to drown his dog, Churchill put his hands over Rufus's eyes so he wouldn't witness such cruelty.

Perhaps it is stretching it a bit to include swans when talking about royal pets, but the Queen technically co-owns all the swans in the United Kingdom. Her co-owners are the Vintners' and Dyers' Livery Companies in the City of London (whose right of ownership dates from the fifteenth century). Prior to that date the sovereign had sole ownership rights to all swans on every stretch of water in Britain, and the birds were considered a delicacy for the royal table.

These days, although the Queen does not eat the

birds, she still exercises her rights once a year by ordering a census of the swan population on certain stretches of the River Thames.

Her interests are looked after by a gentleman who bears the grandiose title of the Queen's swan marker. For generations this office has rested in the Turk family, whose experienced river men know the Thames inside and out.

Apart from marking the swans annually and then reporting back to Her Majesty, the swan marker also looks after the general health and welfare of the birds, rescues any that are injured and arranges for the temporary removal of swans from areas of the Thames during rowing regattas – for their own safety!

If there is one way in which royalty demonstrates its devotion to its pets, it is the manner by which lavish attention is showered on them. Little expense is spared, they sleep in luxurious beds, eat the best food money can buy and receive the finest medical attention. The animals also enjoy unlimited access to their royal owners, a privilege denied to almost anyone else, apart from immediate family and those involved in the care of the animals. Racehorse trainers, veterinary surgeons and, as we shall see, one very special 'horse whisperer' from the United States all form part of this exclusive category.

And it is not a one-way street. Of course, the royal family have their favourites, but their pets have theirs also. The Queen's corgis are hers and hers alone; they are not interested in anyone else. Princess Anne's dogs, when not attacking other animals, ignore practically everyone except her, and she is the only one they obey. The same applies to every member of the royal family. Their pets, from Princess Michael of Kent's cats to the Duchess of Cornwall's Jack Russell terriers, are territorial and ultra-possessive regarding their royal owners.

While certain high-ranking household officials and politicians believe they enjoy a special relationship with royalty, the truth is that only their pets are the real royal family favourites.

3

Rewards for Royalty

For generations, ambitious highborn men and women have attempted to gain favour at court by giving animals as presents to members of the royal family. It is a custom that continues to this day. When the poet Alexander Pope gave Frederick, Prince of Wales, a Great Dane in the eighteenth century, he had a special collar made as a gift on which was written the rhyme: 'I am His Highness' dog at Kew, Pray tell me, Sir, whose dog are you?'

It was the royal dress designer Hardy Amies who, knowing his most famous client's affection for all animals, decided to gain a little extra royal favour by giving her a toy kangaroo, complete with diamond tiara and carrying a bouquet of flowers, for Christmas 1962. The Queen loved it and the kangaroo was given pride of place on the grand piano at Sandringham. Amies added to the gift every year and by 1986 there was a virtual menagerie on the piano.

In Queen Victoria's reign the practice reached an all-time high. She was showered with gifts of dogs including a Scottish deerhound, Hector; a Sussex spaniel puppy, Tilco; a cashmere pug; an Eskimo dog from Captain Wemyss in 1843; and a greyhound, Giddy, which was a gift from Lord Lurgan in 1873. Many gifts were presented by members of the aristocracy who considered it a great honour to have one of their dogs accepted by Victoria. In turn, she accepted the tributes as her right.

Of all the dogs given to Queen Victoria by relatives and foreign royalty, the ones she cherished above all others were the animals she received from her beloved husband, Prince Albert. Perhaps the greatest favourite of all was Dandie Dinmont (this was the name of the dog, now attached to the breed), a present for her 23rd birthday in 1842. The dog lived until 1858, dying at the age of nineteen.

She was also showered with gifts from her extended German family, including: two Hungarian Transylvanian sheepdogs in 1843; a pug, Fermach, from the Crown Prince of Prussia in 1845; Vulcan, a German boarhound; Briach, a mastiff; and two dachshunds, Dalkiel and Waldina.

Monarchs have always liked to exchange live animals as gifts; the more exotic and rare the animal, the greater its value as a gift with the recipient and donor able to display their ostentatious wealth and status. Over the years, British sovereigns have received live cheetahs, giraffes, jaguars, sloths and even an elephant.

The President of Cameroon celebrated the Queen and Prince Philip's silver wedding anniversary in November 1972 by offering them a seven-year-old bull elephant called, of course, Jumbo. He was found quarters at the Children's Zoo at Crystal Palace where he became a great favourite, before being moved first to Regent's Park Zoo and finally to Whipsnade a year later. In 1961, President Tubman of Liberia made a state visit to Britain and on his return home he sent two pygmy hippopotami as a gift to the Duke of Edinburgh, which were immediately presented to London Zoo on permanent loan.

In 1968, during the Queen's state visit to Brazil, she was given two sloths and in Gambia in 1961, she was offered – and accepted – a baby crocodile named Mansa ('king') for Prince Andrew. The Queen's private secretary, Sir Martin Charteris, was ordered to keep the reptile in his private tin bath until it was time for the flight back to Britain where, after Andrew had viewed his new pet, it too was dispatched to London Zoo.

The five-year-old Princess Anne received an unusual gift from the two Soviet leaders Bulganin and Khrushchev in April 1956 in Nikki, a three-month-old brown Syrian bear. No one knew if they expected the pet to be kept in the garden at Buckingham Palace but in any case it ended up in Regent's Park Zoo with details of its progress sent to the Palace regularly. And Anne was thrilled when Nikki sired four cubs and wondered why she couldn't keep at least one of them in her room.

It was during the same visit that Khrushchev and Bulganin presented Prince Philip with a magnificent stallion, Mele-Kush, called simply Mele in the stables. Mele was a headstrong animal that needed firm handling. He was ridden only by His Royal Highness, one of the more experienced grooms or occasionally by some of the Queen's male guests, if they fancied the challenge.

One year later it was Prince Charles's turn to be the recipient of an especially unusual present. Goldie, a dark brown stag from the municipality of Rapperswil in

Switzerland, was given to mark the 250th visitor under a reciprocal holiday exchange between certain London boroughs and their opposite numbers in Switzerland. The prince was also given a small stallion, Zaman, when he was just eight years old.

On a state visit to Austria in 1969, the Queen was presented with a beautiful pair of the country's famous Haflinger mountain ponies, which she brought back to Scotland where they joined her Highland and fell ponies, which were used as deer and working ponies on the estate.

Valentine, a bay gelding, was given to the Queen by Queen Beatrix of the Netherlands. He was found a comfortable home in the royal mews where he was ridden every day by one of the grooms.

Other equestrian gifts to the royal family included Sutton, who was given to the Queen in 1959 by the then President of Pakistan, and Bussaco, a present from the President of Portugal in 1957.

For the man who appeared to already have every-thing, there was only one possible gift suitable for the Prince of Wales when he celebrated his 21st birthday on 14 November 1969 and the Royal Warrant Holders

Association came up with the perfect present: a splendid polo pony called Pecas. Charles was delighted with it and he rode it frequently in matches on Smith's Lawn, Windsor.

London Zoo has been the happy recipient of several of the Queen's more unusual gifts, including a canary from Germany, a couple of black beavers from Canada and two young giant turtles from the Seychelles, along with the aforementioned elephant, which came from Cameroon. Most of Britain's zoos have reason to thank the royal family – and their generous donors – for giving (or lending) them some of the more exotic animals in their collections.

To receive a gift of one of Her Majesty's animals is a mark of her personal esteem, and among grateful recipients have been President Valéry Giscard d'Estaing when he was France's head of state and also King Juan Carlos of Spain, who was so delighted with his presents from the Queen that he has successfully bred from the yellow Labradors she gave him.

Among the many different and exotic animals given to Edward VII as Prince of Wales and as monarch was a Pomeranian, Beaty, a gift from the Tsar of Russia.

When he paid a visit to Ireland in 1903, his host, Lord Dudley, presented him with an Irish terrier puppy that he brought back to England. He also received a chow-chow from the brother of his private secretary, purchased from a captain in the Indian army, who had carried it from the Far East, a journey of more than 10,000 miles.

Queen Victoria's Pekingese, Looty, also came from the Far East, this time from China in 1860. It too was a gift from an army officer who had 'released' it from captivity in the Summer Palace where it was found in the private apartments of an aunt of the emperor. Until the nineteenth century, only the Emperor of China could own pekes and anyone else who was seen with one in his or her possession was sentenced to be stoned to death in public. Back in England, Looty (sometimes spelt Lootie) lived happily in the Windsor kennels until 1872, but there is no record of Queen Victoria ever visiting her newest foreign pet. Queen Alexandra was also given a Pekingese, this time as a birthday present by tycoon Alfred de Rothschild. She named the dog Xerxes.

In more recent times, the Duke of Kent (late father of the present duke) gifted his daughter, Princess Alexandra, first cousin to the Queen, a superb chow-chow, who boasted the elegant pedigree name of Choonam Li Wu T'song, but was always called by the young princess by its pet name of Muff.

The extended royal family have become used to receiving animals as gifts, particularly during their travels to foreign parts. The present Countess Mountbatten of Burma remembers when her mother, the wife of Lord Louis (later Earl) Mountbatten, came home from India with a lion cub named Sabi. It was given a home in the room of one of the younger servants over the estate garage. As it happened, the cub turned out to be a gentle and harmless creature, but when it eventually grew to maturity and was too large to share a bedroom with the servants, it was sent to Dudley Zoo, where the poor animal pined and died shortly afterwards.

Lady (Edwina) Mountbatten was a great animal lover, who went everywhere accompanied by her two Sealyham terriers, Mizzen and Jib. She also had a honey bear – actually a kinkajou native to Central and South America but sometimes kept as an exotic pet in other parts of the world – while her husband, the last Viceroy of India, turned up one day with a mongoose named Neola, which became the treasured pet of his younger daughter Pamela (now Lady Pamela Hicks). Lady Pamela recalled to the present author how Neola came to be hers.

My father was given the mongoose when we arrived in India and he wasn't too keen so he 'off-loaded' it on to me. I was eighteen at the time and we took to each other straight away. Neola, the name simply means 'mongoose' in Hindustani, became one of the most widely travelled mongooses in the world as when our time in India was up we took Neola with us to Malta and then back home to England where he enjoyed a long and peaceful life until he died at Broadlands [the Mountbatten home in Hampshire].

Lady Pamela also remembers the Sealyhams, her mother's pride and joy.

> One sadly died just before we left for India and my mother, believing the other would not survive quarantine, decided to take him with us. Remember, this was 1947 when Britain was still in the grip of postwar austerity. Food and everything else was rationed and dogs were usually fed on scraps. However, on our arrival in India at the Viceroy's palace, a servant appeared carrying a silver tray on which was displayed a dish of pure white minced chicken breast, something we had not seen in Britain for many years. My mother said it was far too good for the dog, and promptly ate it herself. The servant was then despatched to find something more suitable for the canine palate.

It was Lord Mountbatten who gave the young Princess Elizabeth one of her most exotic gifts. Home on leave from one of his foreign postings during the Second World War, he brought with him a scaly, lizard-like creature that turned out to be a chameleon, and presented it to Elizabeth and her sister. They were delighted with the creature, particularly when Princess Margaret placed it on a copy of *Debrett's Peerage* which was coloured red and the chameleon immediately turned the same shade. Both Elizabeth and Margaret liked to carry the reptile in their hands, to the dismay of their governess and other members of the household. And one of their favourite tricks was to place him on the window sill in the dining room where the bluebottles gathered and watch his long black tongue snake out and capture one to eat.

The newest member of the royal family to receive a gift of a pet is Catherine, the Duchess of Cambridge. She was given a black cocker spaniel named Lupo by her mother, Carole Middleton, who breeds cockers. Prince William has a beautiful black Labrador, Wigen, a gift from the van Cutsem family who are old friends of the Prince of Wales.

The practice of sending gifts to royalty continues to this day. In 2012, the Queen was the recipient of a number of animal-related presents. These included a bed for her corgis in the shape of a crown; the adoption rights to a baby Asian elephant (no one explained to her exactly what 'adoption rights' meant); a baby llama, which was dispatched to a new home in a zoo; and a knitted tea cosy bearing Her Majesty's likeness, surrounded by corgis.

The Princess Royal was also on the receiving end of several gifts that year, with one in particular coming in handy. It was a horse blanket destined to keep her personal mount comfortable on cold winter days.

If a member of the royal family receives a gift from someone they do not know, before they accept it (and everyone receives an acknowledgement whether it is kept or not) their officials make enquiries to see if the donor is 'suitable'. There have been instances of people and organisations sending expensive gifts to royalty simply for the publicity. Rarely are these gifts sent anonymously and frequently a 'leak' to the media accompanies the present. When this occurs, the gift is invariably returned and a note is made in the household files so that should the exercise be repeated, it too will be refused. Royalty is not above accepting expensive gifts, particularly anything to do with animals, but only if there are no strings attached!

4

Corgis Rule OK?

The place of corgis in royal life is exemplified in the *Royal Encyclopaedia*, the official and authoritative book on the royal family. The section devoted to corgis warrants twenty-nine lines, whereas that detailing the duties of palace footmen is given only eighteen lines.

Whenever Her Majesty is being fitted for clothes in her special apartment at Buckingham Palace, she carries a small magnet with her and then, even at her age, goes over every inch of the room, picking up any stray pins and needles so they don't harm tiny paws. Every one of the Queen's dress designers, from Hardy Amies to Angela Kelly, the present 'keeper of the royal wardrobe', has been made aware that the corgis take pride of place and no harm must come to any of them.

On one occasion one of the corgis started bleeding badly from a cut paw and was obviously in a lot of pain. The Queen had just returned from an engagement and was fully dressed in an immaculate outfit. Regardless, she tore up strips of material from one of her pillow cases and bound the wound herself after gently rubbing some of her own ointment on the cut. Within days the injury had healed; it didn't need the attention of one of the royal veterinary surgeons. Her Majesty even treats her dogs with her personal homeopathic medicines, saying, 'If it's good enough for me, it should me good enough for them.'

Throughout their reign as the Queen's favoured pets, the corgis have been the most pampered pooches and over-indulged pets in the land. Not terribly imposing to look at, standing barely twelve inches high with short, stumpy legs, no tail to speak of and enormous ears, corgis are very agile and quick on their feet. Legend has it they were used to guard against wolves in previous centuries, though the idea of a small dog challenging a bigger, wild ferocious beast does seem rather far-fetched. They are also intensely loyal to their owners and highly intelligent.

There are two types of corgi: Pembrokeshire (which is what the royal family keeps) and Cardiganshire. They can be recognised by the fact that the Pembrokeshire has a short tail, practically a 'bob', while his opposite number from the adjoining county sports a long, bushy tail. Both breeds were employed to herd sheep, hence their tendency to nip at unwary ankles or snap at dangling hands, as several seated guests at luncheon parties have discovered to their cost.

The corgis are an essential part of the Queen's family. She would be lost without them and they go everywhere with her. They move from home to home, travelling in royal limousine, helicopter, aircraft and the royal train – and, until 1997, aboard the royal yacht *Britannia*, which the dogs apparently loved despite being wary of the ship's cat. At Sandringham, when the royal family gathers for the festivities, they each have their own Christmas stocking, filled by the Queen with all the little bits of food and sweets they like. Chocolate drops are the firm favourite, but they no longer receive any squeaky toys as they used to. These days the noise drives Her Majesty and her guests to distraction.

Her Majesty's sitting room is located on the first floor of Buckingham Palace and in a drawer in her desk she keeps a dog brush handy so that if she has a spare moment in the day, she can groom her pets herself. She does not allow any of her footmen or housemaids to handle the task, which is just as well, as they are all very wary of getting too close to the animals.

Corgis are social animals but as with any of us there is a strict pecking order. Her Majesty's senior dogs are all aware of their standing and status and any newcomer is soon made to know his or her place. They know it, the Queen knows it and, indeed, she encourages it; after all, life in the kennels only reflects the social order of her own family above stairs where everyone knows their place, and keeps to it.

The Queen's corgis can be summed up in a few short succinct sentences. First, they are small, but with comparatively long canine lives. They are practical and tough, keen watchdogs, very perky and extremely good family pets, which seems a bit of a contradiction when one hears they are prone to nipping at strangers. They enjoy the company of humans, but not necessarily other dogs. They are adaptable and are excellent for both town and country living and do not have a high exercise requirement. Their tough, short coats need little maintenance; they are quick to learn but need strict controlling – which they get from

Her Majesty – as they tend to be self-willed. In other words, they have to learn who is boss. The Queen's dogs are very bossy by nature and are trained with a firm but gentle hand, otherwise they will take over.

There has never been a chance of this with the Queen as their mistress. She follows the golden rule that one should not treat corgis as toy dogs. Their origins as working animals has ingrained in them the instinct to make up their own minds, such as when they were herding cattle or sheep, and they do not like to be neglected or left too long on their own as this is when they get up to mischief, chewing everything in sight, as the housekeepers at Buckingham Palace, Windsor Castle, Balmoral and Sandringham can confirm.

The Queen's life is planned around a number of 'Fixed Feasts', duties and occasions in the calendar that do not change from one year to the next.

There's Christmas at Sandringham, with the decorations remaining up until 6 February, the day her beloved father died and she acceded to the throne (obviously Her Majesty is not superstitious about taking the decorations down on Twelfth Night). Then she returns to London to begin the working year.

A Saturday in June, usually but not always the second, marks Her Majesty's Official Birthday, when she takes the salute on Horse Guards at the annual Trooping the Colour Parade.

And later in June, the court retires to Windsor Castle for a week and the Queen and her house guests attend the Royal Ascot race meeting religiously every afternoon.

August and September are invariably spent at Balmoral Castle in the Highlands of Scotland, when the Prime Minister of the day and his or her partner are invited for one weekend.

November means the State Opening of Parliament, with the Queen reading a speech word for word written for her by the Prime Minister, outlining his government's proposed legislation for the coming parliamentary year.

Throughout the working year, on a weekly basis, the Prime Minister is received in audience every Tuesday evening at 6.30 p.m. for an informal discussion on matters of state. It used to be 5.30 but when the children were small the Queen liked to spend this time with them and she changed the time to half past six. For some reason nobody has thought to change it back.

And every day, summer or winter, there is one little ceremony that takes place without fail at 5 p.m. and with undeviating formality. It is the time when Her

Majesty's dogs have their evening meal and nothing, affairs of state, Prime Minister or President, is allowed to interfere with this most important event in the day.

Members of the royal household all know when feeding time takes place and they understand they are not to disturb their royal employer under any circumstances once the bell has been rung in her sitting room to signal the dogs' meal time.

A liveried footman is summoned by the Queen's page, Paul Whybrew, her most senior domestic servant, and together with a uniformed housemaid he lays a green plastic sheet over the carpet in the corridor immediately outside Her Majesty's sitting room.

Metal bowls, so highly polished they are often mistaken for silver, which the Queen is anxious to point out they are not, each one inscribed with a dog's name, are placed in a row outside the 'little palaces' the dogs call home.

In all it takes some seven people to cook, prepare and serve the daily meals for the dogs, and it has for over sixty years: a clerk, the royal chef, a kitchen operative, a housemaid, a page, a footman and Her Majesty herself.

A daily menu for the corgis, typed on headed writing paper by a Palace clerk, is posted on the kitchen wall.

Each day it varies. One day it might be boiled and diced steak, served with rice and finely chopped cabbage. The next day it could be poached chicken and the next liver. Occasionally, at Windsor, Sandringham or Balmoral, a choice rabbit, shot by Prince William or Harry on the estate, might be on the menu – with all the shot and bones removed, of course.

The proud boast is that none of Her Majesty's animals has ever eaten anything out of a can. The minced steak is the finest fillet and only pure white breast of chicken is cooked. But there is one extra ingredient that has to be added.

Palace legend has it that the Queen knows of a secret formula for special gravy, known only to her, which is added to the meal and mixed into a large bowl before she measures each portion into the individual bowls.

Once the royal chef has seen the menu for the day, he supervises the preparation of the food and then it is carried by a kitchen operative (they used to call them porters but no longer) to the green baize door that separates the kitchen from the Palace proper. But he is not allowed outside the kitchen so he hands the food over to a footman, who then carries it upstairs to the corridor outside the Queen's sitting room. There, he hands it over to Her Majesty's page, who, under the watchful eye of the Queen, fills the feeding bowls.

The dogs can, naturally, smell the food and they become very excited in anticipation. But they are, on the whole, so obedient that none attempts to eat before being given the command by the Queen. And this being royalty, they are fed in order of seniority.

Occasionally, discipline has been known to break down when one of the animals cannot wait and tries to jump the queue. When this happens, the footman moves in quickly and picks up the offender and makes him wait his turn. This can be the risky part of feeding time as footmen have been known to be bitten by the dogs, which are snappy little creatures at the best of times, as the staff all know. But servants know they must never reprimand the dog, on pain of instant dismissal from the Palace. One footman who was bitten decided to get his own back by adding a large drop of gin and whisky to the dogs' food, causing them to act very strangely. When the Queen found out she was furious and the master of the household had to use all his diplomatic skills to prevent the man from being discharged. Instead he was demoted to a lower grade and not allowed anywhere near the animals again – for which he was duly grateful.

If it is a particularly fine day, Her Majesty may decide to move the entire feeding operation out of doors where the meals are served on the rear terrace. At tea time in the Palace, liveried footmen serve warm scones, jam and cream, but the Queen does not eat any; instead she feeds them all to the dogs. No wonder they are overweight!

Now that the Queen's pack of dogs has been reduced to just two corgis, Hollow and Willow, and two dorgis (cross-bred corgis and dachshunds), Candy and Vulcan, all four of whom are no longer in the first flush of youth, they are generally well behaved and they do not have the fights that use to break out when Her Majesty had a dozen or so to manage.

The extraordinary thing is that as the animals are so obedient and respond to the Queen's every command when it is meal time, she has not bothered to make them fully house trained. The staff keep a supply of blotting paper and soda water on hand just in case of little 'accidents'. And when they are taken in the garden at Buckingham Palace for a walk after they have eaten, towels are stored just inside the doorway of the garden entrance (it is on the Constitution Hill side of the Palace and easily recognisable as it is the only one with bow windows) so that the footmen can dry any muddy paws. Cleanliness is obviously important; hygiene not so vital.

The dogs all recognise the Queen's voice and they appear to be able to sense by her tone what sort of mood she is in. Some people who claim to know her well say she is more comfortable with animals than people. But that is a remark often made about animal lovers.

The Queen has an acute sense of humour and she loves a good joke, even a slightly risqué one. But there is one subject on which she will never share a joke and that is her corgis. They are strictly off limits, as more than one guest has discovered to his cost. One gentleman, attempting to find common ground with Her Majesty, joked that his corgi liked to beg, just like hers, only to be sharply reprimanded with the words, 'My dogs do not beg.' End of conversation.

And a young Guards officer, attending his first official meal with the royal family and seeking to break the ice, tried to tell a story about a corgi that was cooked in error in a French restaurant, only to be met with a stony silence.

Although the breed is naturally aggressive, the Queen's breeding programme has been said to have reduced their 'snappiness' to the relief of family and household staff, not all of whom are convinced. Of course, no animals belonging to the Queen would 'snap' and neither would she tolerate the slightest criticism from any quarter. A guest at Sandringham suddenly found himself out of favour after uttering the mildest scolding to one of his hostess's animals. He was discreetly urged by a member of the household to 'discover' he had just received notice of urgent business elsewhere. He immediately left the house party after making his excuses.

One former footman at Sandringham was knocked unconscious while leading nine corgis on leashes; the animals rushed down the steps and they all ended up in a tangle on the floor. Of course, it was the poor footman who got the blame.

Few of royalty's guests are prepared to voice their dislike of their pets, even if, privately, they loathe them. One noted exception was the celebrated actor, playwright, raconteur and possessor of an acerbic wit, Sir Noël Coward. As the story was told by the Queen Mother's long-serving page, William Tallon, Sir Noël was a great friend of all the royal family. During one of his early visits to the Queen Mother at Clarence House, she could see he wasn't too enamoured of her corgis. So she asked him why. 'Because, Ma'am,' he replied, 'they are fat, spoilt, snappy and they stink.' It was the first – and only – time anyone had dared to express such an unfavourable opinion of her beloved little treasures and she left the room for a few moments.

While she was out Sir Noël said that the dogs, 'sensing my distaste, kept their distance and eyed me with a mixture of disdain and rancour. Which I returned in full. All except one, who tried to be playful by seizing my trouser leg. I quickly discouraged him with a sharp little kick and he retreated to a corner – and sulked.' The Queen Mother returned to the gathering and resumed the conversation as if Sir Noël's remark had never been made.

The Princess Royal has been heard to reply waspishly to anyone who has had the temerity to utter any comment, even jokingly, that might imply the mildest criticism of her mother's animals.

Even junior members of the royal family have to be careful not to complain about the dogs. Lord Snowdon tells of the time his son David (Viscount Linley, whose mother was Princess Margaret) was visiting his grandmother, the Queen Mother, at Clarence House when a small boy. Her favourite corgi at the time, Jack, suddenly leapt up and bit him on the face, drawing blood. The boy, naturally hurt and frightened, complained to his grandmother but she just dismissed the incident: 'He was only playing.'

The Queen has always had a blind spot where her dogs are concerned, even with her late mother. The Queen Mother's own pack of corgis did not get on at all with those owned by the Queen. They often fought when the two packs were together at Balmoral and, when that happened, the Queen always laid the blame squarely at the door of her mother's animals: her own could do no wrong.

Henry Kissinger, former United States Secretary of State, is a good friend of the Queen and Prince Philip and in 1995 Her Majesty awarded Dr Kissinger an honorary knighthood for his services to international diplomacy. He told me a little story concerning one of the Queen's pets.

The Queen was most gracious and gave me a lunch

at Windsor. It was during the meal that Prince Philip saved me from making what could have been a faux pas.

Towards the end of lunch the Queen's corgis came in and sat at her feet. Now I am very fond of dogs – in fact, I regard myself as a 'dog nut' – and for the moment I forgot where I was, calling across the table to my wife, Nancy, who was sitting next to Prince Philip, 'Look what's sitting under the table.' There was complete silence and everybody – there were around forty of us present – stopped what they were doing. Prince Philip jumped to my rescue, making a remark about them being the bane of his life and everyone laughed. He had said it in a joking fashion that defused the situation straight away and I was very grateful.

Her Majesty loves her own dogs to distraction but, contrary to public belief, this affection does not extend to other people's animals. In fact, she is not in the least bit interested in seeing or hearing about dogs other than her own, with the possible exception of working dogs. Occasionally, on visits, she is greeted by well-meaning local Pembrokeshire corgi groups, all expecting her to be as enthusiastic as they are. She tries to appear interested and her innate good manners prevent her from showing her true feelings. Again, with guests at luncheons or dinners, she does not encourage discussion about the relative merits of her dogs as they wander about the room, sniffing for titbits that fall from the table. Other people's opinions do not concern her; she is a possessive 'parent' to her corgis and dorgis and she knows all she needs to know about their breeding and habits.

Visitors to Buckingham Palace soon become aware that the corgis are the Queen's private pets and she does not like to see anyone else, even members of her own family, touching them.

Quite often the first indication that guests have that the Queen is approaching is when they hear a scampering of little paws and the corgis appear. One or two unwary guests have tried to pat the dogs, only to be told sharply by Her Majesty to leave them alone.

When the world-famous Welsh singer Katherine Jenkins was a guest at the Palace, she decided to get down on the floor and play with the corgis when she saw them. She was lucky; they didn't bite her. It was reported that the singer later said that when she looked up she found she was on a level with the Queen's knees. Her Majesty's reaction has not been recorded.

5

The Corgi Dynasty

The Queen's first corgi was Susan (Hickathrift Pippa), an 18th birthday present from her parents. Susan would become the founder of what was to be a royal corgi dynasty. Her Majesty has owned over thirty corgis since Susan and every one has been bred from that foundation bitch, making the Queen the only corgi breeder in the United Kingdom whose breeding can be traced to the original animal. Susan had three puppies, Sugar, Jane and Honey, with Sugar then giving birth to Whisky and Sherry, while Honey became mother to Bee and Buzz. Sugar, who was born in 1949, lived until 18 July 1965.

At Christmas 1955, Whisky was a surprise present for the seven-year-old Prince Charles, while Sherry went to his five-year-old sister, Anne.

The breeding continued with Heather, who was born in May 1961 and became a great favourite, particularly when she gave birth to a litter of three: Tiny, Bushy and

Foxy. Foxy gained favour when she produced Brush in 1969, followed by Shadow and Smokey. Heather lived to be nearly sixteen, dying in January 1977.

Tiny was mated with Pipkin, a dachshund belonging to Princess Margaret, with Clipper, Piper and May the result. When Her Majesty was asked how a short-legged corgi could be mated with an even shorter-legged dachshund, she replied, with the straightest of faces, 'We stand one of them on a brick.'

Susan was prone to biting anyone who came within range. Her target on one notable occasion was a royal clock winder, Mr Leonard Hubbard, who needed hospital treatment after she took a massive bite out of his leg.

In 1959, Susan received another black mark when she bit a policeman on duty at Buckingham Palace, having already bitten three other Palace employees: a sentry, a member of the Palace police force and the royal clock winder.

As a breeder of corgis, the Queen is a 'hands-on' owner, preferring to be present when they give birth and often helping with the messy bits. But the breeding programme has never been for profit. The Queen does not sell any of the puppies. She has given some to good homes, but rarely to other members of her own family as she knows they do not all share her love for the breed. When Princess Michael of Kent was said to have remarked that she sometimes felt like shooting them, the Queen is alleged to have replied, to the person repeating the comment, 'They're better behaved than she is.'

And it is widely known that Prince Philip is not a fan, once exclaiming, 'Bloody dogs! Why do you have to have so many?'

It was the Queen Mother, then the Duchess of York, who first introduced house dogs – as opposed to gun dogs – into the present royal family as she had grown up with dogs as pets from early childhood.

Her mother-in-law, Queen Mary, on the other hand, refused to allow any animals inside the royal residences, including Buckingham Palace, insisting that only gun dogs should be kept and outside in kennels, as they were at Sandringham and Balmoral. It is believed that her dislike of house dogs arose from the fact that her mother-in-law, Queen Alexandra, was surrounded by dogs of all breeds and sizes and insisted on allowing them free rein in palace and castle without regard to hygiene or cleanliness.

Corgis were a little-known breed outside Wales back in the 1930s when the royal family acquired the first of their dynasty. In fact, they were recognised as a breed by the Kennel Club only in 1928. Just three years before only ten corgis had been registered with the Kennel Club. By the time Elizabeth II ascended the throne, they had become the second most popular breed in Britain with their registrations being counted in their thousands. In the 1960s more than 10,000 registrations were received at the Kennel Club. By 2011 the pendulum had swung the other way once more with just 333 Pembrokeshire registrations recorded and even fewer, a mere ninety-four, in Cardiganshire. Two other favoured breeds, however, Labradors and cocker spaniels, soared in popularity with some 36,000 registrations for Labradors alone. In the year of Her Majesty's Diamond Jubilee and the Olympic Games, however, the popularity of corgis increased dramatically once more.

The corgis love being the centre of attention, so when the Queen agreed to take an active part in the opening ceremony of the 2012 Olympic Games, three of her pets greeted James Bond (a.k.a. the actor Daniel Craig) and escorted him to Her Majesty's apartments, where they hogged the camera and practically stole the show.

In September 2012, shortly after the games ended, the oldest of the trio, thirteen-year-old Monty, died at Balmoral. He was a good age for a corgi; the lifespan is usually between eleven and thirteen.

Monty was not named after the famous wartime soldier, Field Marshal Viscount Montgomery, as was generally supposed, but after Monty Roberts, an American old friend of the Queen, who advises her on both horses and corgis. He offered to replace Monty with one of his own dogs, but the offer was gently declined on the grounds that Her Majesty did not wish to expand her pack of corgis at her age.

Monty had all sorts of little idiosyncrasies, including chasing squirrels in the gardens at Buckingham Palace. He never caught them as they ran up a tree to escape every time. But Monty thought they were his playmates and enjoyed his romps around the garden.

The Queen has commissioned several portraits of her various favourite animals including the springer spaniels and the dorgis.

After featuring in the television coverage of the opening ceremony of the Olympic Games, the corgis were immortalised in a portrait of the Queen that has been installed in a window at the Queen's Chapel of the Savoy, which has been the official church of the Royal Victorian Order, the sovereign's personal order of chivalry, since King George V commanded that it should be so.

The artist commissioned by the Duchy of Lancaster (Her Majesty is Duke of Lancaster, not Duchess, in spite of her gender, and in this right she owns the Chapel of the Savoy) to carry out the work to mark Her Majesty's Diamond Jubilee was Scotsman Douglas Hogg, who beat off competition from more than thirty other artists to secure the prize. The portrait is based on the official seal of the order and shows the monarch mounted on a horse in the garb of a medieval knight. Hogg said that he was told that the Queen had altered the position of the horse's legs in the portrait, commenting, 'She had also added a corgi. It is excellent because it makes the work more personal and powerful. There is not much she does not know about horses, of course. A dog also jumps up at the horse's foreleg.'

When the Duchy of Lancaster was asked for a comment on the inclusion of the corgi, a spokesman said, 'We believe that this change was made when the Queen's seal was commissioned. Her Majesty added a personal touch of a corgi beneath the horse's hooves.'

The magnificent stained-glass window, which also depicts the Queen's sixty-year reign with the dates 1952 and 2012 featured around the royal cypher EIIR, was unveiled by Her Majesty on 1 November 2012.

An earlier portrait of the Queen's dogs was a much more informal picture and was painted by a self-taught artist, Cindy Lass, who has for many years raised money through her work for Battersea Dogs and Cats Home. In 2001, she completed a series called 'Celebrity Pawtraits', which included the animals of Sir Elton John, George Michael and Cate Blanchett, and was asked to travel to New York to do the same thing for President Bill Clinton and the actress Shirley MacLaine. On returning to the United Kingdom in 2003, Cindy received an unusual summons. 'I was just back when I had a phone call from one of the Queen's ladies-in-waiting, asking if I would like to paint Her Majesty's corgis. Of course, I said yes and I was anxious to do it in time for the Queen's 80th birthday.' Cindy explains what happened next:

I was sent a photograph from which to work as there wasn't all that much time, and I was puzzled that some of the dogs looked different to the others. So I rang the Palace and was told that some were 'dorgis'. I had never heard of this breed, so they explained that they were cross-breeds mated with corgis. I then went on to complete the picture which was 5ft x 4ft acrylic, painted on canvas.

Cindy spends part of her time at University College Hospital in London teaching children who are suffering from terminal cancer to paint in a form of therapy that helps them forget their pain for a time. When she had finished the painting of the corgis, Cindy rang the Palace to ask if some of the children might accompany her when she delivered it.

The lady-in-waiting said that of course they could come, so I hired a bus and an ambulance followed us with a couple of children who were not well enough to travel by bus. One of the Queen's footmen met us and we all had photographs taken at the Palace, which was a real treat. The next day I received a call to tell me that Her Majesty had liked the portrait so much it had made her smile and it was now hanging in her private apartments.

Cindy was also given permission to use the likeness on tea towels and T-shirts, which are sold with the proceeds donated to the Dogs Trust.

The royal corgis have been commemorated in a number of different ways. The Queen Mother memorial bronze, which can be seen in The Mall in London, shows her with two of her corgi pets.

Statues, stamps, stained-glass windows and various other works of art have each included a corgi alongside members of the royal family. The crown coin which was minted to mark the Queen's Golden Jubilee in 2012 shows her with one of her pet corgis.

Visitors to St George's Hall in Windsor Castle will see a cast-iron fireback which was the idea of Sir Martin Charteris, one of the Queen's earliest and most devoted private secretaries. He was an enthusiastic and accomplished amateur sculptor who began the fireback as a tribute to Her Majesty, but was unable to finish it before he died on 23 December 1999. A young sculptor at Eton, where Sir Martin ended his career as provost, completed the work. Among the usual royal emblems featured on the fireback one will spot a trio of corgis.

It is not only in the United Kingdom that the Queen's affection (or is it passion?) for corgis is recognised. In 1983 when she and Prince Philip visited Grand Cayman, government officials presented her with a black coral sculpture of a corgi, which delighted her, and a similar work of art, depicting a horse, went to Prince Philip.

Welsh corgis, both Pembrokeshire and Cardiganshire, have been bred to be used as working dogs, as exhibition show dogs or simply as household pets.

The Queen has deliberately kept all her corgis as personal pets. At the same time she has instigated a breeding programme emanating from Susan which has evolved into producing animals of physical perfection. They are good enough to be exhibited in the show ring, but Her Majesty has chosen not to allow them to be entered, unlike her working gun dogs, who have not only entered many field trials but have been consistently successful in them.

The corgis owned by the Queen may live a life of luxury far removed from the farms of west Wales where they originated, but they still retain the natural intelligence and working qualities for which the breed has been known for hundreds of years.

The Queen has demonstrated that her dogs are all the better for not being shut up in kennels but allowed to roam at will, wherever she is: palace, castle or at Sandringham.

She believes that corgis are among the most intelligent of dogs and that leaving them to mix freely with humans – albeit, not always with unqualified success – contributes to their character-building programme.

So, why did the Queen choose corgis when historically the breed has traditionally been considered to be the favoured companions of men, not women? Obviously, this relates to their former role as working dogs, able to spend hours on end out of doors in all winds and weather. The corgis' short, wiry coat does not require regular trimming and even when soaking wet they are easy and fast to dry.

One thing that immediately appealed to the Queen (or Princess Elizabeth, as she then was) is their size. Weighing on average around twenty pounds and small in stature, they don't take up too much room. And a plus factor is that they do not, apparently, suffer from travel sickness, either in cars, trains, aircraft or helicopters. A final point in their favour is that corgis like to stay close to their home base; they do not tend to wander or run away, unlike many other breeds.

The Queen's corgis are as much at home in the centre of metropolitan London as they are in rural Norfolk or even the tough hillside country surrounding Balmoral. This is another of the attractions of the breed; they are equally adaptable to town and country. Wherever they are, though, they do always need regular exercise. Because of their size, corgis are sometimes imagined to be lapdogs and little else. This is a complete fallacy. They are also extremely valuable as guard dogs, not perhaps through their ability to attack or even repel intruders, but to give warning. Any sign of an unwanted stranger means loud and consistent barking, which is usually enough to warn off all but the most determined – and foolish – invader.

And although they are said to be 'snappy' little dogs, because their natural instinct is to herd sheep and cattle, they do not normally break the skin when they bite. It's more of a gentle 'nip', which was all that was needed when they were used as working dogs in the fields. But try telling that to the men and women at the Palace who have been bitten by one of them! Just about everyone in Palace circles knows about the corgis' propensity to 'nip' at heels and ankles, sometimes from personal experience. One such is the Queen's most senior lady-in-waiting, her mistress of the robes, the Duchess of Grafton, who was bitten by one of the dogs only to be reassured by Her Majesty that their mouths are so soft that they don't even break the skin. They did give the duchess a nasty fright, however.

In the seventy years the Queen has owned corgis they have become her trademark, along with her 'dorgis', those cross-bred corgis and dachshunds she is so fond of. It was the late Diana, Princess of Wales, who coined the phrase 'a moving carpet' to describe the wave of small dogs that precede Her Majesty wherever she goes. But with only four dogs left it could hardly be described thus today; maybe not a carpet, just a little rug.

The late Queen Mother was asked why members of the royal family are so devoted to their animals and she replied, 'Because they always forgive one.' She might also have added that it was partly because of their no-nonsense attitude. Corgis are notorious for refusing to come to heel when commanded, so perhaps it makes a nice change in the family where nearly every request is treated as if it were a papal benediction.

When the Prime Minister is received in audience by the Queen every Wednesday evening (it used to be Tuesday, but for some unknown reason it was changed during the Blair years) he or she is greeted by the sight of the monarch with her dogs at her feet and they stay throughout the meeting. If only dogs could talk. And at official luncheons and dinners they are never very far away. In fact, the only formal occasions when they are kept confined to their own quarters are at the investitures and state banquets. And this is not because they might get in the way, but for their own protection when there are so many strange legs and feet moving around.

The Queen likes to judge people, particularly if they are going to work for her, by their attitude to her animals. A former communications secretary was being given a final interview by the Queen before she confirmed his appointment when one of the corgis kept tugging at his trouser leg. Her Majesty appeared to take no notice of the incident so the interviewee ignored it also, in spite of the fact that he was probably longing to kick the little horror. Anyway, he got the top job, and later it was said that it was partly his ability to stoically endure the distraction that gave him the royal seal of approval.

The Queen rarely expresses her feelings or emotions face to face with anyone, except perhaps the Duke of Edinburgh. But she can, and does, write her thoughts down.

When one of her favourite corgis died, Lady Pamela Hicks, who was lady-in-waiting when the Queen was still Princess Elizabeth (and a bridesmaid at her wedding) and who has remained a firm friend ever since, wrote her a note of condolence, only to receive a six-page handwritten letter in reply telling Pamela of the deep feelings she had for the dog. It was a very moving letter and revealed emotions the Queen would never have stated in person.

When one of her mother's dogs died during a shooting weekend party at Sandringham, Her Majesty visited each of her guests before dinner that evening and gave them the news personally after Prince Phillip had tried to comfort her.

Wherever the Queen has gone during her long reign, her dogs have accompanied her. In the mid-1970s she was often seen at Windsor, Balmoral or Sandringham surrounded by two of her Labradors, Harvey and Sherry, with her cross-bred dorgi Tinker and her corgi Brush never far away.

As Prince William matured, he found it difficult to share the enthusiasm for corgis held by his grandmother and great-grandmother. He said one of the reasons was that they never seemed to stop yapping and their tendency to snap at everyone, which amused the Queen and the Queen Mother, merely annoyed him.

As Duke of Cambridge, William recently said, perhaps only half-jokingly, that one of the changes he will make when he eventually succeeds to the throne is to get rid of the corgis. 'They bark all the time,' he said, but not within hearing distance of his grandmother. Of course, he would never do or say anything to upset her during her lifetime, but there may have been more than a little truth in what he said.

♦

As previously stated, the Queen has owned more than thirty corgis in her lifetime, with the largest number at any one time being seven in 2002. They were Emma, Linnet, Rush, Minnie, Monty, Willow and Holly (see Appendix 2). In addition, there have been eight dorgis at different times: Harris, Brandy, Cider, Berry, Tinker, Pickles, Chipper and Piper.

The Queen used to allow each of her corgi bitches one litter. She never sold the puppies but after careful vetting, she would give away the dogs she was not going to keep – but only to good homes after they had been investigated and proved to be suitable.

It was in May 2009 that the Queen said she was not going to continue breeding corgis as she had done for over sixty years. What caused this momentous decision was the deaths of four of her half-a-dozen dogs, leaving her with just two. It is truly the end of an era but Her Majesty would prefer the dynasty to come to a natural end.

6

All the Queen's Horses

'A horse, a horse, my kingdom for a horse!' This may well be the most famous phrase associated with any monarch and the discovery early in 2013 in a car park in Leicester of the remains of King Richard III, the monarch who uttered the immortal appeal (though there is no evidence that he actually ever said those words – they were put into his mouth by William Shakespeare in his play of the same name), may seem singularly appropriate when one examines the equestrian influence of royalty through the centuries.

If it appears to be perfectly natural that the present generation of the royal family grew up in the saddle, perhaps it is not too surprising when one looks back at their history.

Members of the royal family, from the Queen to her youngest grandchild, are taught to ride almost as soon as they can walk and even at the age of eighty-seven Her

Majesty still rides every weekend at Windsor – though she refuses to wear a hard hat.

Princess Anne was fitted for her first set of riding boots, made by Lobb of St James's at a cost of £100, when she was three years old. Her first pony was called Bandit though she had to share it with her brother Charles until she was given one of her own, High Jinks, on her 12th birthday. Charles had already been given Fum, his first Shetland pony, which became a favourite pet until the young prince grew too big for the tiny animal. When Princess Anne was ten years old she was seen driving a light pony and carriage in the grounds of Windsor Castle. The carriage originally belonged to her great-great-grandmother, Queen Alexandra.

Undeniably the most accomplished royal horsewoman of her generation, Anne, before she became the Princess Royal in July 1986, won the European Three-Day Event Championship in 1971 on one of the Queen's horses, while Zara Phillips won both European and World titles and then competed in the 2012 Olympic Games, winning team silver medal. And both mother and daughter have ridden in races wearing the Queen's colours.

Members of the royal family rarely show emotion in public – or even to each other. They regard it as a private matter and a weakness. In fact, the only time the Queen and Princess Anne have been known to shed tears in public was when one of their favourite horses died. No one has ever seen any of them cry for the loss of a human being, even a close relative. Animals and personal possessions are different. At the decommissioning ceremony of the royal yacht *Britannia* in 1997, the Queen was said to have 'blinked rather a lot' – which was the nearest admission they got to public tears.

Of all the horses associated with the Queen, the most famous and easily recognisable was Burmese, the last of fifteen horses Her Majesty rode at the Trooping the Colour Parade throughout the years.

It was in 1969 that the Royal Canadian Mounted Police presented the mare to the Queen when they came to Britain to perform at the Royal Windsor Horse Show. Burmese was seven by the time she arrived in Britain and she took part in the Trooping the Colour Parade that same year.

A niece of the then crown equerry, the late Lieutenant-Colonel Sir John Miller (he was knighted by the Queen in 1974 and made a Knight Commander of the Royal Victorian Order), a great friend of the royal family, used to ride Burmese for a few hours leading up to the ceremony, in order to tire her a little and calm her down if necessary.

Her Majesty rode Burmese at every Trooping after that first occasion, until the horse was deemed to be too old and retired following the 1986 ceremony. It was then that the Queen decided that she did not want to have a new horse trained in place of Burmese, so a horse-drawn carriage has been used to convey her to the ceremony ever since.

During her visit to Regina, Canada, in 2005, the Queen unveiled a statue to Burmese, who died in 1990 at the age of twenty-one.

In June 1981, the Queen was riding Burmese to the annual Sovereign's Birthday Parade – which is the correct name for what is commonly called Trooping the Colour – when they were involved in what could have been a fatal incident. A young man suddenly stepped out of the crowds on the corner of The Mall and fired six shots at her before he was overpowered. As it happened, the shots were blanks but no one knew that at the time. Fortunately, no one was injured but Burmese was naturally disturbed by the noise of the shots and reacted accordingly. The Queen didn't even flinch. Her iron self-control took over and she calmed the horse and carried on to the parade as if nothing had happened.

Burmese was the last in a distinguished line of fine horses ridden by the Queen at the Sovereign's Birthday Parade. It was in 1947, when she was just twenty-one and still a princess, that she first rode side-saddle in the parade. Her mount on that occasion was Tommy, a bay hunter. Before the then princess rode him he was specially prepared for the formal parade by an understudy who rode him to several railway stations in London to get him accustomed to the noise and clatter. The understudy was Mrs Archer Houblon, a vastly experienced horsewoman who also took charge of Tommy at the two rehearsals held on Horse Guards before the big day. He behaved perfectly.

It was also one of Mrs Houblon's tasks to help Princess Elizabeth become more proficient in the difficult art of riding side-saddle: how to maintain her equilibrium while controlling her mount with only one leg as opposed to both when riding astride. She would arrive at the royal mews a full month before the Birthday Parade and coach her royal pupil in how to control the animal. She would also school both Tommy and one other, as there is always a replacement ready in case of injury to the first choice. The princess was no novice, however, as she had first received instruction in side-saddle riding during the early years of the Second World War when she was taught the rudiments by Horace Smith at the Holyport stables in Berkshire.

The parade went off without a hitch but the following year's was cancelled owing to bad weather. In 1949 King George VI was not well enough to ride his usual horse, so he attended the parade in a carriage while his elder daughter rode alongside him on his horse Winston.

In 1950 the King again rode in a carriage but Princess Elizabeth did not attend the parade as she was expecting the birth of her daughter, Princess Anne, who arrived on 15 August. The following year His Majesty was again unwell and did not attend the parade so the princess took the salute, once more riding Winston. The chestnut-coloured police horse became the princess's mount at Trooping the Colour for the next four years.

So, in 1952, 1953 and 1954, Winston was the Queen's horse but in 1955 there was no Sovereign's Birthday Parade owing to a national rail strike. However, Her Majesty did ride Winston again in 1956.

At the Coronation, Winston was ridden in the procession by the Metropolitan Police commissioner. Sadly he had to be painlessly put down following a fall at the police mounted training establishment at Thames Ditton on 7 February 1957.

It was the Metropolitan Police Force that provided

Winston's successor. Imperial was bought in Yorkshire as an unbroken three-year-old, before being sent to Imber Court where the Met train their horses. Imperial was ridden by the Queen from 1957 to 1962 and again in 1964 and 1965. In between, in 1963, a horse named Doctor was chosen to carry the Queen and he was on royal duty again in 1966. The following year, Her Majesty rode Neill to take the salute at the parade and Fairway completed the troop of horses ridden by the Queen in 1968 before Burmese took over from 1969 to 1986.

Few spectators at the Sovereign's Birthday Parade realised that the animals the Queen used to ride were in fact working police horses who were used every day on patrol in the busy streets of London, and who could also be seen in crowd control action at football matches.

If horses figure largely in the history of the royal family it is perfectly understandable. The tradition of equestrian excellence is as established as the monarchy itself, and the idea of any prince or princess not being familiar with horses is as unthinkable as the Queen riding a motorbike around London. The Queen, the Duke of Edinburgh, the Prince of Wales and the Princess Royal all treat their horses as personal friends and when they were children their ponies became their constant companions.

All the horses owned and ridden by the Queen are not just animals to her but individual characters, each with its own peculiarities and foibles in which she takes a great personal interest and pleasure.

Among Her Majesty's great favourites are several who have become pets, including Betsy, who was bought in the Queen's coronation year and who remained in the Windsor mews for more than twenty years. A beautiful black/brown mare, she loathed being clipped and would always make life difficult for the grooms when they tried. In her later years she also loved to have a quiet nap in the afternoons and woe betide any unwary stable lad or lass who dared to disturb her slumbers. Anyone who woke her suddenly was likely to get a nasty nip.

Agreement was another who became a favourite at Windsor. He was a former racehorse, having won the Doncaster Cup as a four-year-old, but when his days on the racecourse were over he was brought to Windsor where the Queen once described him as 'rather a sad horse, with rather a sad history'. One of his pet hates was that he refused to allow any females to ride him, having been ridden only by stable lads and jockeys in his racing career. But Her Majesty loves a challenge and she eventually managed to handle him, once Agreement had been properly schooled by the stud grooms.

In royal terms, Prince Philip was a late starter as a horseman. With most royal children learning to ride almost as soon as they could walk, certainly by the time they were four or five, he did not have his first lesson until he was ten years old. It was when he went to school at Gordonstoun that his teaching continued with two very experienced instructors. He and all the other boys were taught not only to ride but also how to look after their ponies and all the secrets of stable management. They were lessons he remembered all his life and which he insisted his children should also learn.

Prince Philip may not share the Queen's enthusiasm for racing but he does share her affection for horses. In his case polo was his first love as a younger man and even now, at ninety-two, he still energetically supports carriage driving, though he no longer plays an active role. The Queen always supported him when he was taking part at Windsor or Sandringham. Once, when he actually won the event at Sandringham, someone congratulated him and casually mentioned that it was not a bad performance for an old-age pensioner. He was sixty-seven at the time, but he did not appreciate the comment.

What is not generally known is that the Queen was a proficient carriage driver long before her husband. In fact, she won first prize two years running, 1943 and 1944, at the Royal Windsor Horse Show. However, she is tactful enough never to mention this in his presence.

The Queen used to enjoy riding Prince Philip's horses – when he allowed it – one of which was Sultan, a gift to the prince from the President of Pakistan in 1959. Classically bred, among his ancestors was the famous Derby winner Blue Peter. He was said to have a rather 'tempestuous' temperament, but both the Queen and Prince Philip enjoyed the challenge of a somewhat 'stronger' outing.

Pride was a gift to the Queen from King Hussein of Jordan in 1958 and he arrived in Britain as an unbroken stallion. Once he had been trained both the Queen and Princess Anne loved to take him out and when he damaged a tendon, Her Majesty and the princess treated him personally, dressing his injured leg with a poultice for some hours.

Back in the 1960s, Her Majesty rode Bussaco, a present from the President of Portugal in 1957. During Royal Ascot Week, the Queen often suggested the horse as a mount for one of her guests at Windsor Castle who wanted to ride.

Princess Anne favoured Benbow when she was a pupil at Benenden public school. During the holidays she loved to ride the animal at Windsor as long as it wasn't raining – apparently Benbow hated wet conditions and even shied away from any puddles. As schoolchildren, Anne and Charles had two very special horses, William and Greensleeves, and William in particular liked to share their afternoon tea – when their governess wasn't looking.

Princess Anne learned from her mother how important it is to take a close personal interest in the welfare of her horses. It was not enough just to ride them, or even to learn their little mannerisms. If one of the animals was ill or off colour, Anne – as her mother had before her – would visit the stables several times a day to check on its progress.

At Sandringham, there is plenty of opportunity for Her Majesty to ride in privacy and also to visit the stables and paddocks whenever she chooses. There are innumerable rides over the estate and Princess Anne, one of the most experienced riders in the family, reckons even today she can still find areas that are new to her.

Of course, Norfolk is a flat county and when the Queen rides over its windswept fields, she feels the full impact of the near gale-force blasts. Guests who join the royal family on horseback often say (out of their hosts' hearing) that they prefer the comparative calm of the wooded tracks or the shelter of the park at Sandringham.

When Her Majesty is in residence at Windsor – most weekends – the stables are in a state of ever-readiness, all geared up to provide the Queen with her horse whenever she decides to ride. The stablehands will be informed by the Queen's page the evening before of what time she wishes to ride. She is never late. If she says ten o'clock, then she'll arrive at exactly that moment. Punctuality is not only the politeness of princes.

She does not normally mount her horse in the royal mews, but is driven to a point somewhere in the park where the stud groom meets her. He brings her horse fed and watered and in pristine condition.

When riding, the Queen has two magnificent sheep-skins, one pure white, the other black, which fit over her saddle and make for a very comfortable seat.

The Queen likes to ride alone if possible, but she accepts that her personal protection officer has to be near at all times. A groom also rides nearby to open and close the many locked gates in the park using the key that is kept in the royal mews.

When Andrew and Edward were young children they liked to be taken out in the park when their mother was riding. They would travel in an open-sided carriage named Victoria, which was a gift to King Edward VII from the Kaiser. The Queen was once heard to say it was 'just the sort of thing children fall out of'. Luckily they never did.

One of the grooms at Windsor came into the stables one morning to hear the sound of someone singing softly. On investigation, he discovered it was the Queen, who was either serenading her horse or just singing to herself. Either way, the groom crept quietly away and Her Majesty was none the wiser that there had been a witness – not that it would have bothered her in the slightest.

Up at Balmoral the Queen knows all her ponies and their particular characteristics, tempers, likes and dislikes. Even though in appearance they can hardly be compared with Her Majesty's thoroughbreds, these working animals are as much a part of her life as the most valuable of her racehorses.

The Balmoral fell ponies are direct descendants of the pack animals that were used to haul heavy loads from the lead mines of the Lake District to the nearest seaports, travelling over the roughest terrain in all weather, which makes them ideal for the hills and valleys on the 50,000-acre Balmoral estate.

The fell ponies were introduced by George VI, who had been advised that they were just the sort of ponies the estate needed. But they were not welcomed with open arms at first by the 'old guard' at Balmoral, who did not like change and who were used to working with their native Highland ponies. But the King wanted them and the stable staff's loyalty to their sovereign overcame their objections. He was also the person who paid their wages. Today all the ponies are treated exactly the same.

Wishing to breed fell ponies, George VI bought a mare named Gypsy, who became the matriarch of the present fell pony dynasty at Balmoral. It is from her that all subsequent fells have descended, including a couple of Highland/fell crosses.

The Queen's grandchildren, when they were small, loved the ponies, thinking that because they were so tiny compared with the horses in the royal mews, they would be that much easier to ride. Charles and Anne, when they were very young, loved going to Balmoral in the summer where they rode the ponies every day. To them, these working animals were regarded as pets.

Even today, whenever Anne is at Balmoral, which is part of every summer when the court is in residence, she would not dream of spending a day without at least a couple of hours in the saddle – but, naturally, not on one of the tiny ponies anymore. As the most experienced international horsewoman in the royal family, with her competition days long gone, these days she can ride whenever and wherever she likes, purely for relaxation. And she still likes to ride alone whenever possible, through the woods and across the moors. She is just like her mother; she regards solitude as a privilege to be enjoyed not endured.

Occasionally she will be invited to join the Queen for a ride when they can chat about family matters, but when that happens Anne knows they will not be entirely alone as the ubiquitous police protection officer is always nearby and always within earshot.

Her Majesty has equal feeling for the wide variety of horses she owns, rides and uses in public life, including those in the royal mews whose duties include pulling the state carriages she travels in. When the Queen visits the mews she will always take with her a handful of biscuits to feed the horses as she walks among them and even today she still knows the name of every one of them.

The Queen has been presented with examples of superb animals by fellow heads of state and, advised by her long line of crown equerries (among others), she has also acquired lots of horses for different uses. There are the deer ponies in Scotland, the polo ponies ridden by the male members of her family at Windsor and even some little horses of more modest origins for her children and grandchildren to ride when they are being taught the rudimentary skills of horsemanship.

When she was just three years old, Elizabeth was given her first pony, a docile and shaggy Shetland called Peggy who was stabled in the royal mews at Windsor. The pony did not cost very much; royalty, then as now, loved a bargain, and those early purchases for Elizabeth

– and later for her sister, Margaret – were not expensive. In fact, one was bought for just twenty guineas, which even in those pre-war years was considered to be cheap as only the well off bought their offspring ponies and larger horses. For the working classes, the only horses they saw were those that pulled delivery carts.

Elizabeth was four years old when she attended her first hunt, the Pytchley, on her pony, Peggy. The little pony was an easy ride for a child, but otherwise there was nothing remarkable about her.

Another acquisition was George, an unusual addition to the royal stables in that he was originally a pit pony, working deep underground at a colliery in Durham.

King George VI and Queen Elizabeth saw the animal just before he was about to be lowered to the coalface with the rest of the miners on shift. Princess Elizabeth's mother expressed her admiration for George, especially when she discovered his name, and the pit owner (this was in the days long before nationalisation) – as she knew he would – immediately presented George to Their Majesties as a gift for their young daughters. For generations, royalty has mastered the knack of 'admiring' an item, whether animal or mineral, and then appearing surprised, and delighted, when they are offered the object as a gift.

George was transported to Balmoral, escaping a life of drudgery underground, but his pit training had not equipped him for life as a royal pet. He was obstinate and had a bad habit of walking in any direction he felt like taking, regardless of his rider's wishes. In the colliery, he was used to being left on his own as long as he did the only job he was there for: pulling the heavy coal trams. He was also not the handsomest of creatures and neither princess took to him.

He remained at Balmoral but was reduced to working on the estate, still a better prospect than his previous existence in the coal mines. George was replaced with Gem, who was better behaved but also stubborn, so he too proved difficult for the young girls to handle.

There was a brief interlude while experts throughout the country searched high and low for suitable ponies on which the princesses could be taught to ride correctly – and safely. Then a small docked-tailed Welsh cob named Snowball arrived and he proved to be moderately successful. Like George, he too had had an unusual start in life, having been discovered pulling a jaunting cart in Ireland before being bought by agents on behalf of the royal family and brought over to Windsor so Elizabeth's and Margaret's riding education could continue.

But poor old Snowball suffered from asthma and he was quickly pensioned off when Greylight appeared on the scene. Greylight was by far the best-looking pony Elizabeth was given and her character matched her looks. She was described as the perfect children's riding pony and Elizabeth enjoyed several months with her before she grew too tall for the 12-hands-high animal.

It was when Elizabeth started her serious instruction at the Buckingham Palace riding school that she indicated that riding alone was not enough for her. She also wanted to learn everything she could about the care of horses: their bone structure, diet, hygiene and welfare. Her instructors in the royal mews were told to spare her nothing. If she was going to learn, it was going to be the hard way, with all the heartache that it could cause a young girl. And the King and Queen insisted that both their daughters should get their hands dirty and take their fair share of 'mucking out'. They were not allowed to leave the less than pleasant tasks to the regular stablehands but, in fairness, neither did they try to get out of them. In fact, both Elizabeth and Margaret thoroughly enjoyed this aspect of equestrian involvement.

At the start of the Second World War, the King and Queen sent their daughters to Balmoral to escape the bombing. They didn't live in the castle itself, which had been closed for the duration, but in the grounds in Birkhall, the current Scottish home of Prince Charles and the Duchess of Cornwall.

The teenage Princess Elizabeth seized every opportunity to ride, first on Comet, a 13.2-hand Welsh/Arab cross pony, and later on two rather special ponies: Hans, a pure-bred Norwegian who had only just been broken, and the famous royal favourite, Jock. Neither of the two was the easiest to handle. They both had a tendency to suddenly break into a gallop and also to rear up if they spotted something out of the ordinary. Elizabeth and Margaret were both thrown a number of times but nothing dimmed their enthusiasm for riding.

The ponies absolutely refused to obey any of the Balmoral stable lads, only reacting to Princess Elizabeth's voice. And many years later, when Jock was over twenty years old and had been retired in poor health to spend a comfortable old age at Windsor, he still recognised the Queen's voice when she visited him. Her Majesty later said that Jock had taught her more than any other animal.

Once the royal children have been lifted on to their ponies long enough to get them used to horses, they are taken to the royal mews at Buckingham Palace for proper instruction.

The name 'mews' derives from an ancient French word for feathers as traditionally the sovereign's falcons were kept in this particular place.

There are royal mews at Windsor Castle, Hampton Court Palace and the Palace of Holyroodhouse in Edinburgh as well as at Buckingham Palace, where the thirty carriage horses are stabled in perfect conditions, as well as the state carriages and the royal limousines. The present mews dates from 1825 and, in terms of the layout, not much has changed since then. These days the mews is the scene of one of the most sought-after parties of the year when the royalty protection department (the royal bodyguards) hold their annual Christmas party, which is usually attended by one or two of the younger members of the royal family – with all given strict instructions not to scare the horses!

The riding school where newcomers are instructed adjoins the main mews on the north-west corner, well away from the palace proper.

Prince Charles, Princess Anne, Prince Andrew and Prince Edward were all brought here to receive lessons from one of the most successful crown equerries, Lt-Col. Sir John Miller, who served from 1961 to 1987. A former Welsh Guards commanding officer whose attention to detail was legendary in a household where such matters are usually taken for granted, one of Sir John's greatest tests came at the wedding of Prince Charles and Lady Diana Spencer in 1981. The crown equerry had gone over the route many times, stopwatch in hand, checking and rechecking exactly how long it would take the horse-drawn carriages to travel in both directions. He prided himself on his punctuality and was very distressed when Diana announced that she wanted to exercise her bride's prerogative and arrive at St Paul's Cathedral two minutes late, thereby throwing all his careful plans out of kilter. He was appalled and appealed to the Queen, who told him he would have to compromise. So he allowed the bride to arrive just thirty seconds after the appointed time. She was satisfied, but he later told me that it slightly spoilt his day – and his unblemished record.

The riding school is seventy-five yards long with a firm surface laid on a six-foot deep foundation of faggots and peat. Lt-Col. Miller would make his royal students ride bareback and with their arms folded, controlling the horse only with their thighs. They fell off many times, but as Princess Anne recalled, 'It certainly forced one to concentrate the mind.'

The animals ridden by the Queen and her sister, and subsequent generations of royals, when they were being taught the basic rudiments of horsemanship and later the more advanced lessons, were not selected for their docility. There was instruction from King George VI, and later from Elizabeth II, that it was important right from the very beginning to know how to control horses of varying temperaments in all conditions. As such, staff in the royal mews were ordered to make lots of noise: shouting, banging steel dustbin lids and even playing loud music, with banners being deliberately waved in the horses' faces, both to get the horses used to the row and, more importantly, to enable the young royal riders to learn how to react to any and all conditions. They even had stable lads throwing buckets of water in front of the horses' hooves when Elizabeth and Margaret were riding downhill at Windsor, to get them used to slippery and wet conditions. (They did the same thing on the steep hill in front of Caernarvon Castle in July 1969, just before the investiture of Prince Charles as Prince of Wales). Princess Margaret was a more than competent rider, but Elizabeth was special. She never tired, insisted on going over any aspect of the lessons she wasn't too sure of, and every morning, especially when they were up at Balmoral, she was the first one to be in the saddle.

Both Princess Elizabeth and Princess Margaret were given this sort of instruction with special mounted exercises to improve their balance and confidence. And both proved to be quick learners, graduating to riding without stirrups – it's not as easy as it sounds – within weeks and, shortly afterwards, even jumping small, light fences.

The difficulty for Princess Elizabeth, but not so much for her sister, was that, as it would later be for Prince Charles and even later still, for Prince William, as heir to the throne she could not devote as much time as she would have wished to riding lessons.

Even as a ten-year-old, she was forced to spend hours studying the business of constitutional monarchy, mostly with her grandmother, Queen Mary, who gave her private lessons in geography (so she would know something about the countries she would one day reign over) and also history. Riding had to be squeezed in between.

The Queen has two studs where she breeds horses. At the Hampton Court Palace stud horses are bred for the Household Cavalry and also to pull royal carriages. In Scotland, at the stud on the Balmoral estate, the famous Highland, fell and Haflinger ponies are bred and raised. These are the ponies that have become favoured pets by generations of royal children, mainly because of their size and docility. They are also to be seen taking members of the entrance-fee-paying public around the estate when Balmoral is open to visitors.

'I've wanted to go to the Olympics ever since I could ride,' Zara Phillips, the Queen's granddaughter, says. 'It's special to be selected for your country and I enjoy being part of a team. It would be better to ride in the Olympics or to win a medal for your country than to ride at Badminton. I now realise how much Mum and Dad's achievements mean...'

As the daughter of two Olympic competitors, Zara would seem to have been born to be a champion or bred for the job. Mark Phillips was part of the British Olympic team and won a team gold medal in 1972 and a silver in 1988, while her mother, Princess Anne, became European Three-Day Event champion in 1971, when she was just twenty-one years old, and completed the notorious cross-country course at Montreal in 1976, even after being concussed by a bad fall.

Zara once said she did not want to equal her parents' achievements. 'I want to do better than them.' She certainly started well in her aim to reach the top.

In the space of twelve months she achieved her two main ambitions, surpassing everything her mother and father had accomplished: she won both European and World Three-Day Event titles in 2006. Then in 2012 she represented Great Britain in the Olympic Games in London, winning a team silver medal in the process. At the time of writing she is already preparing for the next games, to be held in Brazil in 2016 – if she is selected, of course. In the meantime, Buckingham Palace has announced that Zara and her husband are expecting their first child early in 2014.

So why did Zara choose this most demanding of sports and within it the toughest of disciplines? The decision to pursue eventing as a full-time occupation, as opposed to merely treating it as a rich girl's part-time hobby, was taken quite deliberately, and in the full knowledge of the amount of dedication and sheer hard work that was involved.

Zara was practically born to the saddle. She cannot remember a time when she could not ride. Both she and her brother Peter started their love affair with horses before their 4th birthdays. They were lifted on to Smokey, their Shetland pony, and led around the Gatcombe estate before either of them had started at nursery school. The grounds at Gatcombe Park are ideal for a young rider to learn to handle cross-country courses before venturing into open competition and once Zara had begun to take her sport seriously, both Anne and Mark instilled in their daughter the discipline she needed to make her mark.

They also liked the fact that she shared their rather 'un-British' trait of hating to lose. The idea of being a good loser when coming second was never an option for them; neither is it for Zara. She is a winner.

Of course, every top rider has to have the best horse and in Toytown (nicknamed Noddy by Zara) she has had the finest. The Queen, the Princess Royal, Mark Phillips and Zara all have equal shares in the horse and they all have a special fondness for him. He is not only a great champion, he is a family pet. Zara says, 'He is a family favourite ... but he's a big baby and needs loads of attention.'

Prince Andrew is another more than competent royal horseman. He was first lifted on to a pony when he was just two years old. A tiny Shetland pony was his first mount, as he trotted along in the royal mews with his big sister Anne.

When Andrew was a very young boy, he would often go missing at Buckingham Palace or Windsor, but nobody was too concerned as they knew where they were likely to find him. Andrew loved the mews and, at Windsor in particular, all the stable staff knew him well and loved to hear his chatter as he visited his father's polo ponies or the Queen's riding horses.

And, when he could persuade them, which was frequently, they would sit him up in front on one of the horse-drawn carriages beside the groom as they exercised throughout the Great Park. As a special treat, Andrew would be allowed to take the reins, carefully supervised of course. He showed no fear, either when helping to drive a carriage or when he was on horseback.

On one occasion, the Queen discovered Andrew in the mews riding his tricycle on the cobbled paths, closely followed by two of her corgis and, keeping a watchful eye, his nursery maid. It wasn't strictly permitted, but Her Majesty turned a blind eye.

As his prowess grew over the years, so too did Andrew. He was a sturdy lad and three larger ponies were brought for him to ride. First there was Valkyrie, then Mister Dinkum and then his first polo pony, a gentle animal called Zamba.

As Andrew and his younger brother, Edward, were the Queen's 'second' family – Andrew being born some ten years after his sister Anne – they naturally became closer to each other than to their other two siblings. Yet, Anne has always regarded Edward as her favourite brother; he is very much the 'baby' in her eyes, even in adulthood.

When they were children, she a teenager and he just four or five years old, she loved to look after him and indulge him in a way that in later years she never did with her own children. He would beg her to play with his pets and she never lost patience with him. When he too started to ride, it was Anne who encouraged him. She would spend hours leading him on his pony, particularly when the family was on holiday at Balmoral, and there was little chance of intrusive media coverage or inquisitive public eyes to see him make a mistake or fall off, which he sometimes did. Anne has always liked to 'muck out' her horses herself and she introduced Edward to this necessary but not always pleasant aspect of equestrian life.

The Queen's nephew, Viscount Linley, like his cousins, was introduced to riding at an early age. At Sandringham, he became so fond of Valkyrie, a Shetland pony that was kept for the smallest children to ride, that he regarded it as his own personal pet. This did not please Prince Andrew, who is roughly the same age as David Linley and who was told by the Queen to take it in turns with his cousin. They occasionally fell out over whose turn it was, but generally they got on pretty well. As Andrew was bigger and slightly older and more experienced than David, he enjoyed showing him how to negotiate the tiny six-inch hurdles used to make them familiar with jumping obstacles. The lessons were well learned as both Andrew and David became more than competent horsemen in later life – as well as retaining their close friendship.

Prince Andrew, Duke of York, has passed on his riding prowess to his daughters, Princesses Beatrice and Eugenie, both of whom, like other royal children, appear to have developed a natural affinity with horses.

The Queen is able to call on the best advice in the world for anything she needs, whether for herself or for any of her animals. When she heard about Monty Roberts, the legendary 'Horse Whisperer' who was based in California and who had a reputation for being able to train any horse, she dispatched crown equerry John Miller to check Mr Roberts out for himself.

At first, Sir John was sceptical and not convinced of Roberts's powers but, after putting him through a series of stringent tests, he changed his mind. 'Her Majesty is going to want to see this,' he said. And see it she did.

Monty Roberts was invited to stay at Windsor in April 1989 and the Queen showed him a number of her young untrained horses. As Mr Roberts recalled, 'I had saddles and bridles on them all in five days.' Monty then became a frequent visitor to Windsor, making up to five visits a year. He worked mainly with her youngest horses and also helped with her racehorses when required.

The routine became similar to that enjoyed with her racing manager; Monty would receive a telephone call from 'The Boss' every evening asking how the day had gone and enquiring if there was any particular problem she should know about.

He said, 'She is a detail person and nothing is too small to mention to her.' She demanded to know every-thing about all her animals and each one's performance.

Mr Roberts added that the Queen never forgets anything and she is 'intensely interested'. Mr Roberts has also been invaluable to the Queen with his advice on her dogs when she needed that little bit of extra knowledge.

Her Majesty recognised Monty Roberts's service to her by making him a Member of the Royal Victorian Order, her personal order of chivalry. However, as an American – or non-British citizen – he received the award in an honorary capacity, which in no way is a reduced decoration, simply that it would be discourteous to offer a citizen of a foreign country a normal British honour. He is still invited to the annual service attended by every Member of the Order and he wears his medal with pride.

The Queen recently asked Mr Roberts if he would be willing to train several of her British-based staff and a number of grooms have visited California on short-term 'crash courses'.

His association with the Queen has also brought Mr Roberts other benefits. Once the relationship became public knowledge, he was inundated with requests for advice and, as he has put it, 'I went global.'

7

The Sport of Queens

The Queen's knowledge of racehorses, their breeding, pedigree and form, is well known among the racing fraternity and she is accepted not just as sovereign but as 'one of us'. Which is how she likes it. The royal family has always been keen on horse racing, some more than others. When the Queen entertains her guests for five days at Royal Ascot, Prince Philip, although honour bound to accompany his wife daily in the obligatory carriage drive from Windsor Castle, down the Long Walk and onto the course (he missed the event in 2013 as he was recuperating from an illness), rarely takes any interest in the racing itself. He says it is one of the most boring sports known to man (it is hardly a sport, more a multi-million-pound business) and, when the races are actually being run, he usually retires to the back of the royal box for most of the afternoon to watch cricket on a specially installed television set.

The Queen, however, is a serious enthusiast about racing and when the late Earl of Caernarvon was Her Majesty's racing manager, he was said to be the only person in the world, including members of her own family, who could reach her at any time, wherever she was.

They used to talk on the telephone every evening and on one occasion the Prime Minister was kept waiting for his weekly audience until the Queen had finished hearing her daily racing report from 'Porchy' – the name by which he was known to his friends and family until the day he died on 11 September 2001 ('Porchy' from his former courtesy title Lord Porchester, which he used until he succeeded to the earldom).

The Queen's ancestors were responsible for starting royalty's fondness for the sport with both Henry VIII and Elizabeth I famous for breeding thoroughbred horses while James I was responsible for founding Newmarket racecourse. But perhaps it was Charles II, once the monarchy had been restored in 1660, who did more for equestrian sport than any other sovereign. He spent every spare hour with his horses and was said to have made Newmarket his personal playground. He fed his string of Arab thoroughbreds on a diet of fresh eggs and bread soaked in good old English ale. After feeding his horses, he liked to join the jockeys in impromptu 'races' across the heath, which he invariably won.

Queen Anne (1702–14) is said to have made an enormous contribution to royal participation in horse racing when she founded the Ascot races in 1711. The Queen had been following hunts in a specially built horse-drawn carriage, which she drove herself at sometimes reckless speeds, when she found herself near what is now the water jump at Ascot. She decided there and then that Ascot Heath would be an ideal place to build a racecourse and history was made. Today her memory is commemorated by the Queen Anne Stakes at Royal Ascot, which has become one of the highlights of the annual racing calendar.

Today, everyone in the racing world knows there are just two places on earth where the finest stallions live: Ireland and the United States of America.

Ireland would obviously have been more geographically convenient when the Queen was looking for stallions to mate with her mares, but the political situation made it difficult for many years. Though there was never a threat against her personally, when considering going there she was advised that her presence might cause difficulties for the Irish studs.

The alternative was America, a country the Queen

knows well, having travelled there in a private capacity – as much as any head of state would be allowed to do – to stay at the home of William and Sarah Farish. Mr Farish was a former US ambassador to the United Kingdom and became friends with the Queen when he was based in London.

Her Majesty enjoyed the comparative informality of life in Kentucky and she attended the famous bloodstock sales – without being able to afford any of the animals on offer. She was thrilled when one of her England-trained horses won the big race of the day at Arlington racecourse.

Another of the reasons why the Queen enjoyed her visits to the USA was that she was able to meet and discuss racing with some of the country's most successful owners and breeders, who, though respectful of her rank and position, were not in the least intimidated by her presence. Racing being a democratic sport where everyone has an opinion, some of the people she met were slightly surprised at Her Majesty's knowledge.

The Queen has been sending mares to the United States for many years. Just after the Second World War most of the best stallions in the world found their way to America and, by the time the Queen came to the throne, she knew she should be thinking of sending a mare or two across the Atlantic. When a mare is sent to America she stays for perhaps three or four years. She is covered by a stallion and any foals she has as a result are brought back to Britain once they have been weaned, to be installed in the royal stud. The first mare to be sent was in the early '60s, with others following during the '70s. Finally in the '80s half a dozen mares went to Alice Chandler at Mill Ridge near Lexington, a principal area for thoroughbred breeding, not only in the United States but the whole world.

As the Queen has been passionate about racing for most of her adult life, she has acquired considerable knowledge of what a racehorse should look like and the points on which they should be judged. She knows the correct shape and pedigree and the lifelines of most of the world's most successful animals, even if she cannot afford to buy them. It is also claimed that she has a fantastic eye for 'form' and if there is a photo-finish to a race she is watching, say at Royal Ascot where the royal box is located right on the finishing line, she is invariably first to offer the correct result.

One of Britain's most successful bookmakers once remarked that he would love to employ her as his 'eyes' so he could find out the names of the winners – and losers – a couple of minutes before the official result is announced and what that might cost him – or earn him – as he would then be able to 'lay off' any unprofitable bets.

Anyone who has seen the Queen at Ascot, either from the crowd or at home watching on the television, has witnessed the obvious excitement she feels during a race. And when one of her horses wins, she is like any other owner or trainer. There is nothing blasé about her and she loves to celebrate.

When Highclere won the French Oaks (Prix de Diane) at Chantilly in 1974, having already given the Queen success by winning the 1000 Guineas earlier that year with Joe Mercer in the saddle, she was ecstatic. On the aircraft flying home she arranged that all the people who had been involved in the victory should be invited to a special celebration dinner party that night in Windsor Castle. Within hours everything was in order. That's the sort of power one enjoys when one is sovereign and has over 300 domestic staff at one's disposal. The toast of the evening was Highclere, named after the ancestral home of the Earl of Caernarvon, Highclere Castle in Berkshire, perhaps today more familiar to millions of viewers as the setting for the popular television drama *Downton Abbey*.

In 1977, Silver Jubilee year, Willie Carson wore the Queen's colours (or silks) of purple body with scarlet sleeves and gold braiding and black velvet cap with a gold fringe when he rode Dunfermline, said to be 'probably the best horse the Queen has ever owned', to win both the Oaks at Epsom and the St Leger at Doncaster. In addition to Pall Mall's success in the 1958 2000 Guineas and Carrozza's triumph in the 1957 Oaks, Her Majesty has won every British Classic – apart from that elusive Derby. Her Majesty traditionally presents the trophy to the winner of the Derby; if she did happen to win it herself, it would be fascinating to see if she presented the cup to herself. When she won the Ascot Gold Cup in 2013, with Estimate, the organisers were faced with just this problem as she normally presents this trophy to the winning owner. On this occasion they came up with the perfect solution: the Duke of York was there that day and he stepped in to present the cup to his delighted mother.

There is one splendid story concerning one of the Queen's trainers who was trying and failing to communicate with a stable lad from Asia. Turning to Her Majesty he asked if she spoke any Indian dialect. When she replied that she didn't, he said, 'Well, you ought to, Ma'am. You ruled the place for long enough.' If anyone else had had the temerity to make such a remark to the Queen his feet would not have touched the floor, but in racing everybody seems to say whatever they like, irrespective of rank. The fact that Her Majesty never ruled over India (the country gained its independence on 15 August 1947, nearly five years before she ascended the throne) simply did not occur to the trainer.

The men and women who act as grooms in the royal stables know that Her Majesty welcomes a chat and they also know that they can tell her what she needs to know rather than what her officials might prefer her to hear. She loves to hear every detail of how her horses are progressing, both mentally and physically. And she also likes the salty humour and vocabulary of the stables. But the lads know where to draw the line, so four-letter words are (usually) omitted from the most risqué jokes.

She recognises all her horses by sight and they appear to know her. She visits the stables frequently and when she does she makes sure she is not wearing any perfume as the smell has been known to overexcite some of the young colts.

It was in 1949 that the young Princess Elizabeth had her first success, with an eight-year-old steeplechaser named Monaveen at Fontwell Park in Sussex. The horse was jointly owned by the princess and her mother, the only time this occurred, and they shared the winner's prize of £204. Monaveen broke a leg in 1950 attempting to jump a hurdle at Hurst Park and had to be put down. It was at the same meeting that Princess Elizabeth won her first race as a solo owner on Astrakhan, a filly that had been a wedding present from the Aga Khan in 1947.

But from the time she came to the throne as Elizabeth II in 1952, her horses raced only on 'the flat' and she never owned horses that went 'over the sticks' so as not to compete with her mother, who always favoured this form of racing and was extremely successful with her string of steeplechase mounts.

Queen Elizabeth the Queen Mother was a great patron of steeplechasing and hurdling, having 457 victories in her racing career. Clarence House was the only private home in London to be equipped with a 'Blower' communication system that carried the results directly from the racecourse to Her Majesty's private secretary's office. He was instructed to relay the results to her sitting room the moment they came in.

When the Queen Mother died, representations were made to the Queen that it would be nice if the royal family could retain a presence in steeplechasing. She agreed and now has a small team of hurdlers and steeplechasers, all of whom are trained by Nicky Henderson at Lambourn. The most successful of her steeplechase horses has been Barber's Shop, giving her eight winners. At the 2013 Royal Windsor Horse Show, the now-retired 11-year-old delighted his royal owner by winning a 'Re-trained' class, for which the Queen received a Tesco voucher as a prize; she was seen to put it in her pocket!

One of the Queen's favourite pastimes during Ascot week was to canter down the course in the early morning, accompanied by some of her house guests, before the crowds arrived. But the media got to hear of it and made it impossible for Her Majesty to enjoy her ride. She steadfastly refused to wear a protective hard hat, as the jockeys have to, preferring a silk headscarf. This inevitably attracted criticism from a certain section of the public – and the media – as does the fact that she won't wear a seat belt even when driving herself on the private roads of her estates.

The Queen is not content to sit back and let her advisers tell her what to buy and when to run her horses. She reads the formbooks and knows exactly what she wants. She also has a photographic memory so she is able to recall events from years past and how one of her horses has performed on those occasions. And in precisely the same way that all her prime ministers have found when they have not done their homework completely, she will soon correct her racing team if she thinks they are wrong and remind them that such and such a horse 'didn't run all that well at York in 1995. Don't you remember?'

And the Queen's prodigious memory is not confined to horses. On a visit to one of her racing studs she saw a familiar face, a groom who had looked after Highclere a quarter of a century earlier. 'Isn't that Betty Brister?' she asked her trainer. And it was.

On the flat, the Queen has around thirty horses in training including: eleven two-year-olds, ten three-year-olds and three slightly older horses. There are also some twenty breeding mares that between them will give birth to up to fifteen foals in a season. Her racing manager, John Warren, who took over the job when his father-in-law, the Earl of Caernarvon, died in 2009, says, 'There is no one in the country, perhaps in the industry worldwide, who has bred more crops of foals.' And she deals with her disappointment if a foal is born and found to be a weakling with the natural stoicism of all racehorse breeders. She says, 'It's all part of the game.'

But as Michael Oswald explained, the Queen is placed nowhere near the top of the major players in the equestrian world.

When the Queen came to the throne, there were thirty or so important owner/breeders in western Europe: Britain, Ireland, France, Italy and Germany. Today very few are left. Probably no more than five or six with the Aga Khan, Prince Khalid Abdullah of Saudi Arabia and the four Maktoum brothers being highly successful, each with around 200 brood mares and a further 250 in training. And there is a huge operation in Ireland, where the Coolmore Stud is based, said to be the largest in the world, which makes them at least ten times bigger than the Queen's stud and in terms of money invested, thirty or forty times larger.

Obviously the Queen cannot match these people in numbers, with all the money that's expended.

The royal studs have always been run as commercial enterprises and they have always paid their way, so it's absolutely right that Her Majesty keeps the whole operation down to stay at its present level and aims for quality not quantity. It's all very well for people to ask, 'Why doesn't the Queen win the Derby?' They seem to forget that in racing terms she is a comparatively small fish in what is now a very large international pond.

There is no doubting the Queen's understanding of her sport. 'She is incredibly knowledgeable,' Sir Michael says,

and one has to be very thorough before, for example, going to one of the Newmarket December sales because she is likely to ask about a particular lot and when you wonder why she should be curious about that one, you suddenly find way back in the catalogue that she has had something to do with the pedigree. She has a tremendous knowledge of pedigrees and not only of her own horses.

The Queen is a very astute owner and investor. One stallion standing named Royal Applause is the stud's biggest single earner and the Queen personally owns part of him. Not the biggest part, but a profitable piece nonetheless. One of the stable lads said it was only the lower part of the left hind leg. Whatever it is, the rest belongs to the Maktoum family. The fee for Royal Applause is around £20,000 and in a season he will cover some 130 mares, so there are total earnings of £2.8 million from that one stallion alone, of which £800,000 goes to the Queen.

One thing that everyone connected with the Queen's racing has to be very sure of is that not one penny comes from the public purse. The Keeper of the Privy Purse – who controls the royal chequebook – heads a small committee at Buckingham Place which meets regularly to make sure there is no overspending. It is an entirely private enterprise and as far back as 1976 the royal stud at Hampton Court was closed to thoroughbreds to avoid any possibility of charges being laid that public money was being used to prop up the Queen's racing activities. If one of the walls surrounding the Hampton Court stud needed repairing or one of the gates had to be painted, the Ministry of Works carried out the job – and paid for it out of public funds. So the Queen's racehorses had to be moved. The royal mews horses could safely be stabled there as they are state horses, but not those owned privately by the Queen or her family. The financial strictures are so severe that even the postage stamps on envelopes used for stud business are paid separately, unlike all other official mail which is stamped with the royal cipher.

But what is the attraction for her in what is a very competitive sport?

Those who work closely with her believe it is an extremely therapeutic exercise. There are always papers waiting for her. Even when she is on holiday at Balmoral or Sandringham, she is never very far away from a private secretary who is likely to pop up with a box full of papers to be looked at and signed. The work never goes away. So racing, which she knows so much about, like her gun dogs, is a subject she can be totally immersed in and which is completely different. She loves to walk around a stud or racing stable and watch horses working and take part in discussions about which horse can mate with which. For two or three hours she can almost, not quite, forget the cares of monarchy. It is very valuable therapy.

So how much time does Her Majesty spend on race-courses? Not all that much. In fact, there are only seven days in the year that are ring-fenced in her diary for racing. First is the Derby, then the five days of Royal Ascot and the Saturday of the King George VI and Queen Elizabeth Stakes. Those are the only immovable dates in the royal racing calendar. Any extra days are all really a matter of luck and have to fit in with where she is and what her duties are likely to be. If she happens to be at Windsor and has a horse running, or is somewhere close and accessible to places such as Newbury, Sandown or Kempton, she might go, but it doesn't happen very often. If she does have a horse running on a day when she is unable to be present or follow the results, a recording of the race is made available to her so she can watch it later. And as she is now competent in the use of her own computer, she is able to keep up to date with all the results from wherever in the world she happens to be.

Her advisers are expected to offer their very best opinions to the Queen but she will certainly reply in no uncertain terms if she disagrees with what is said. An adviser has to make a good case and she will always allow it to be presented. She gives a fair hearing. But if she thinks the adviser is talking absolute rubbish, then she'll say so very firmly. The ultimate decision is always hers; it has to be.

The Queen likes to name all her horses herself. The Princess Royal once said her mother was rather innocent in some ways and she occasionally has to have it pointed out to her that a name she has selected might not be suitable if a double entendre can be found. The Queen Mother used to say to her, 'Oh. You can't have that one. Imagine how it will sound when the commentator says it out loud.' One of the names Her Majesty had to be persuaded not to use was 'Stick it up 'em', for obvious reasons.

Although the Queen has had a racing manager, trainers and now both National Hunt and flat-racing advisers, she has never employed any single royal jockey as such. All the greats have ridden in her colours: Lester Piggott, Sir Gordon Richards and Joe Mercer, who gave the Queen one of her early Classic winners when he rode Highclere to victory in the 1000 Guineas in 1974 and also won the French classic Prix de Diane. So it was a profitable year for Her Majesty as her horses won over £140,000 that season. Willie Carson, Harry Carr and

Doug Smith have also all ridden for her but none has been described as *the* royal jockey. The reason is that the first or senior jockey at whatever stable the Queen is using is usually the man who rides for Her Majesty.

In fact, there are only two people who can be accurately called *the* royal jockey and they are the Queen's daughter, the Princess Royal, and Zara Phillips, her granddaughter, who is the most recent generation of royalty to don the Queen's colours. The Princess Royal has ridden wearing the Queen's silks many times and when she rode was a very capable – and ultra-competitive – amateur. Her first outing was in 1985 over the Derby course at Epsom, when she rode in aid of one of her favourite charities, the Riding for the Disabled Association. Her mount was named Against the Grain and although she was beaten into fourth place she was bitten by the horse racing bug. As she later told me, 'I thought that would be my first and last race.' However, on 5 August 1986 she rode her first winner. The race was at Redcar and Anne's horse was Gulfland. After that there was no stopping her and she notched up a further five winners with ten second places and many lesser places. She soon decided that there wasn't enough excitement on the flat and turned her attention to National Hunt Rules. Her first ride was on Cnoc na Cuille at Kempton Park, coming fourth, and on 3 September

1987 riding at Worcester she achieved her only success, beating the odds-on favourite by half a length. She went on to ride in forty races but never again won. Her old friend Brigadier Andrew Parker Bowles says she took up racing because of the excitement. 'She has always liked the physical aspect of racing, the danger and the challenge ... and she wanted to prove to herself that she could do it.'

Like most owners, the Queen has had mixed fortunes on the turf. As decades go, the '50s were extremely good, the '60s less so. The '70s were highly successful with four classic wins, the '80s and '90s pretty fair. As previously mentioned, 1974 was a good year, as was 1977, when she won both the Oaks and the St Leger, and as far back as 1957, she was the leading owner in the country. But there have also been lean spells when she has gone through several seasons without a major winner. Of course in recent years there has been a vastly increased infusion of overseas capital, which in turn has led to greater international competition. The Queen takes it all in her stride. For her, although winning is a bonus of course, she is a true believer in the Olympic ideal that it is the taking part that is important, in spite of the fact that she has a totally professional attitude to her favourite sport. But there is little possibility of the Queen, or any other member of the present royal family, emulating the successes of Her Majesty's great-grandfather King Edward VII, who owned not one but three Derby winners, the final one being Minoru, who was victorious for his royal owner in 1909, with Herbert Jones as jockey.

The Prince of Wales has never followed racing with the passion attributed to his mother and late grandmother. His equestrian preference was always for polo, just like his father. But he did ride as an amateur, wearing his own colours of scarlet, royal blue sleeves and a black cap, in six races in the 1980s, coming second on Allibar in a handicap at Ludlow, and being unseated twice in five days from his own horse, Good Prospect. After that he was rarely seen on a racehorse and in 2004 his colours were removed from the register as they had been used so rarely.

His wife, the former Camilla Parker Bowles, has been a devoted racegoer for most of her adult life, along with her first husband, Andrew Parker Bowles, who still accompanies his old friend the Princess Royal to race meetings and who once said that Anne was a much better rider than her brother.

It came as something of a surprise in 2005, therefore, shortly after Charles and Camilla married, when they decided to jointly buy a racehorse of their own. Charles had never before given the slightest indication of his intention to become an owner. But as he apparently can deny his wife nothing, it seems he was persuaded to join her in this new enterprise.

The horse, named by the duchess as Royal Superlative, was found at the Sandringham Stud and was worth over £100,000. But royalty never reveal the amount they pay for horses – or anything else!

The Princess Royal is the only one of Her Majesty's family to really share her devotion to horse racing, though Princesses Beatrice and Eugenie certainly appeared to be enjoying themselves at Royal Ascot in 2013. The others put in occasional appearances as dutiful children and grandchildren, but they do not really relish a day at the races as she does and they never go if she is not going to be present.

And this is one of her concerns, that when she is no longer there, no one else in the family will carry on the royal tradition of supporting horse racing in Britain. Though the Prince of Wales loves polo, as do his sons, William and Harry, none of them has as yet shown any interest in owning and breeding racehorses, either 'on the flat' or 'over the sticks'.

In all probability there will always be some sort of royal presence at Royal Ascot and the Derby, but many people involved in the sport feel it will be a sad day indeed when the *Racing Post* ceases to be required daily reading at Buckingham Palace.

8

Polo for Princes

By the time Prince Charles was four years old, he was already a confident young pony rider. Ten years later he took up the sport that was to become an over-riding passion for many years.

Polo had been introduced to Britain in 1871 when the first match was played on Hounslow Heath between two army regiments, the 10th Hussars and the 9th Lancers. Its officers had learned the game while on duty in India. In 1881, Prince George (the future Duke of York and King George V) had also had his first taste of polo during a visit to Buenos Aires, then, as now, the home of some of the world's leading players.

Lord Mountbatten had his first brief and not too successful game of polo in Jodhpur (from where the name of the famous riding breeches comes) in 1921. He was accompanying the then Prince of Wales on his official tour of India when a player did not turn up for a game and Mountbatten was invited to take his place. He had never been on a polo pony before but he was game for anything so immediately he agreed. He later admitted that he hardly touched the ball throughout the entire game but his passion for what was to become a lifetime love affair began.

Lord Mountbatten took up polo again during his time in India as Viceroy and, on his return to Britain in 1948, he introduced Prince Philip to the sport. Philip was a natural; aggressive, fearless. It was when Philip and the then Princess Elizabeth were living in Malta, during his naval posting to the island, that he was able to indulge in the sport and he never lost his affection for it. With everything that Philip takes up, he gives his all. Polo was no exception.

When the couple returned to the United Kingdom, Philip, with the increased encouragement of Earl Mountbatten, became a serious player. In 1955, he agreed to become a founder member of the Household Brigade Polo Club, which later became the exclusive

Guards Polo Club at Smith's Lawn, Windsor, where the entrance fee for non-officers is £22,000 in addition to the annual subscription fee of £5,850. If you are a professional player with a suitably low handicap, the fee drops to £3,150.

Prince Philip has been president of the club, described as the most prestigious polo club in the world, since its formation, while the Queen is its patron. It was Prince Philip who brought polo to the attention of the general public when he opened the Sunday afternoon matches on Smith's Lawn to everyone. Spectators poured in; many, of course, simply in the hope of catching a glimpse of members of the royal family, which they always did. But the result was one that Philip welcomed: a wider appreciation of the sport he loved.

Polo is an expensive sport and it is an extravagance enjoyed only by those with the wherewithal to pay for the string of ponies (at least six are required), the equipment and the team of grooms who support the players.

When Philip began playing in England there was an

outcry from some quarters about the amount of money it was costing from the public purse. In fact, Philip was paying his own way, but it would not be unreasonable to suppose that the Queen may have helped a little in those early days.

One of Philip's major expenses was replacing polo sticks – they cost £100 each. As a competitive and aggressive player, he tended to break more than his fair share in every chukka (phase of play). In addition, as polo ponies suffer injuries during a match, his veterinary bills for treatment and medicines were astronomical. Then money had to be found for stabling and feed and if he had tried to use the facilities of the royal mews there would have been even more of an uproar.

Philip's prowess on the polo field soon elevated him into the top half-dozen or so of the nearly 500 polo players in Britain. As previously stated, polo players from Argentina are acknowledged to be the best in the world and they care little for the rank of other players on the play – which is exactly the way Philip wanted it. He neither gave nor received any quarter, and the other players respected him for it. The sport also helped to keep him fit until arthritis, brought on through breaking so many bones, forced him to give up active involvement. But he refused to abandon equestrian sport altogether and took up carriage driving, a sport some would suggest can be equally demanding.

When Prince Charles was preparing for point-to-point racing he went into a strict training regime to make sure he was fit enough. One of his daily exercises consisted of riding non-stop for half an hour on his bicycle from which the saddle had been removed so he had to stand on the pedals all the way.

In 1979, he proved what a good sport he was by riding a camel in a race at the Royal International Horse Show at Olympia. He said later that the most difficult part of the whole experience was actually trying to get up on to the animal's back. Eventually ladders were found for all the riders and in the race itself Charles finished a creditable third. The event was held to raise funds for the 1980 Olympic Games in Moscow but, as it happened, the British equestrian team did not compete because of the Russian conflict in Afghanistan (a boycott had been urged by the United States President, Jimmy Carter) and neither did the hockey or yachting teams, although the athletics team did send over 100 competitors.

Prince Charles, like all serious horsemen and women, has suffered his fair share of injuries. In 1981, shortly before his marriage to Lady Diana Spencer, he was competing in the Grand Military Steeplechase at Sandown Park. Watched by his fiancée, his grand-mother, Queen Elizabeth the Queen Mother, and his aunt, Princess Margaret, he misjudged a fence and was thrown heavily, landing on his shoulder, which was badly bruised; he also received a bloody nose. But again, like other jockeys, he simply shrugged off the injury, saying it was all part of the game. The incident certainly didn't put him off the sport.

He also took up cross-country riding, a dangerous and exciting pastime where the competitors ride over rugged terrain littered with difficult obstacles. It was the sort of challenge he relished, eventually forming two chaser teams of his own: the Duke of Cornwall's and the Earl of Chester's, both subsidiary titles of the Prince of Wales, until it was pointed out to him that, as heir to the throne, he should not take unnecessary risks. In this

matter he was following in the footsteps of his predecessor as Prince of Wales, the late Duke of Windsor.
The future Edward VIII was a fearless rider both when
hunting and in the more competitive point-to-point
races he enjoyed. But, as heir to the throne, there was
concern about his safety, from Parliament and from the
King and Queen. The whole affair reached its climax
in 1924 when the prince was riding his horse Little
Favourite at a point-to-point meeting at Arborfield in
Berkshire. He rushed the first fence, mistimed it, fell
and was severely concussed. Enough was enough and his
father ordered his son and heir to not take part in any
future steeplechase events. The prince was disappointed,
but the King's word was law and he had to abide by the
rule. However, he was clever enough to notice that he
had not been forbidden to hunt – the King himself was
an enthusiastic rider to hounds – and Edward continued
to hunt regularly in Leicestershire with his brothers. He
also played polo with abandon, if not the same amount
of skill shown much later by Lord Mountbatten, Prince
Philip, Prince Charles and Princes William and Harry.

It was Philip and Mountbatten who urged Charles to
take part in polo, not that he needed much urging, and

he developed a tremendous enthusiasm right from the start. He was given two polo ponies, La Quininia and La Sombra, both experienced in the game, who taught him, as he later claimed, everything he knew about polo. He said, 'She [La Sombra] was a marvel.'

Being a member of the royal family meant he had the funds to finance his purchases of better – and thereby more expensive – ponies and Lord Mountbatten undertook his initial coaching. Although it is not supposed to be, polo is very much a contact sport, and Charles became noted for his willingness to take on the toughest opponents.

He played in Australia when he went there for a short period during school and by the time he went up to Cambridge University – where he was awarded a half-blue (not quite making it to the full university side, which would have meant a full blue) – he had already taken part in his first tournament at Smith's Lawn, his team beating that of the more experienced side captained by Major Ronald Ferguson, father of the young lady who was to become Prince Andrew's wife.

Charles became such a passionate polo player that he found time to play a match against Spain just three days before his marriage to Lady Diana Spencer in 1981. It was in this match that two of the players met head on and collapsed on the ground, unconscious for several minutes. After coming to, they got up and continued to play the game. Charles became such a keen player that he felt a week was wasted if he had not had at least two or three matches. But because of his other royal commitments, he was never able to devote as much time to polo as his father had when he was younger, and it was also claimed that one of his weaknesses was the fact that he lacked the aggression and brutality that characterises the truly great, world-class players. Spectators, who do not all understand the game, sometimes criticise the players for treating their ponies too harshly. And while it is true that veterinary surgeons are always on hand to treat serious injuries, some of the ponies do look in a sorry state at the end of a chukka. Still, Charles became an accomplished polo player achieving a handicap of three at one time; his father was a five in his heyday; some of the South Americans are tens.

As president of the Cambridge University Polo Club, Prince Charles has written an open letter to be included on its website, telling of his passion for the sport.

I have the happiest memories of playing polo whilst I was at Cambridge even though, in my day, we found it quite hard to beat Oxford! Nevertheless it was fun trying all those years ago – over forty to be precise.

Polo is a very challenging sport, demanding riding skills and a good eye for the ball. But, above all, it is the personal teamwork which must be developed between the rider and his pony which is so essential. Polo ponies cannot be treated like motorbikes. Hours of practice always pay handsome dividends.

Polo is without doubt the best team game in the world. There are countless examples where a weaker team on paper can, with good team work, defeat a potentially stronger foe, so do not despair! I can recall several games where we achieved success by doing just that!

9

Anyone for Hunting?

Every member of the royal family, male and female, has hunted at some time. But as hunting is now illegal in Britain, due to a law introduced during Tony Blair's premiership, members of the royal family have abandoned their support of the activity. Previously all of them, particularly Princess Anne, were enthusiastic followers, often hunting two or three times a week; even the Queen, when she was Princess Elizabeth, enjoyed the chase.

As a young girl, the then Princess Elizabeth hunted occasionally with the Pytchley Hunt in Northamptonshire. This was at a time when hunting was considered a normal – even essential – part of any well-to-do young lady's country upbringing. However, the Queen has not hunted since ascending to the throne in 1952.

Prince Charles, no mean performer on horseback, though never in the same league as his sister Anne or more recently his niece Zara Phillips, enjoyed hunting when he was younger, joining the Belvoir (whose pack was owned by the Duke of Rutland) and Cotswold hunts, and the Quorn. Aware of the sensibilities of those who opposed the sport, he usually joined the others long after they had started to avoid any undue publicity. As a countryman he grew up well used to the fact that animals are there to be killed, either as food, to control numbers or simply for recreation. But in later years, it was revealed that he always felt a certain sympathy for the fox and wasn't altogether unhappy when it got away from the pack.

He was a fearless cross-country horseman and often he partnered his favourite strawberry roan hunter mare, Reflection. Wearing his distinctive garb of the 'Windsor Coat' of navy blue with crimson collar and cuffs and gold buttons, which was designed just for him but which was derived from that first worn by his ancestor King George III, Prince Charles was a welcome visitor at all the most fashionable hunts in the country including the Bicester and the Beaufort.

Not all the horses Charles rode when hunting were owned by him or the Queen. He often was offered a loan of some of the finest hunters in the country. In the early days of his hunting career he formed a partnership with Candlewick, owned and bred by the Queen, and later with Mulberry Star, owned by the aforementioned Sir John Miller. Yet another was Highlight, owned by a supporter of the Quorn. Highlight became such a favourite of the prince that one year when Charles was out of the country, he sent the horse a personally signed Christmas card.

It would have been unusual if he had not started riding to hounds, as all his family did, but in adult life he let it be known that he was well aware of the reservations of some sections of the public to foxhunting. However, he has not thought it necessary to air his personal views in public. But he has made comments about the attitude of country folk to hunting, as opposed to those brought up in urban areas. In Michael Clayton's excellent book *Prince Charles: Horseman* (1987) the prince was quoted thus:

I believe it is necessary to have some form of control over the fox population because otherwise everything becomes completely out of hand. I know some think that it is cruel to inflict that kind of pursuit on an animal. But having seen the way foxes operate, I think the good thing about organised hunting, is that at the end of a hunt there is either a dead fox or a perfectly all right fox. There is nothing in between, in the form of a wounded fox. If you trap them, or shoot, or poison them, the kind of death you inflict can be slow and horrendous.

In fairness, it should be emphasised that Prince Charles made these comments some years before legislation was introduced banning the sport. Since the ban, he has not voiced an opinion either way.

The Duchess of Cornwall hunted from a young age and continued to participate in the sport until she was forced, as were many others, to abandon it by law. She is a courageous horsewoman and her affinity with her own horses has been admired by her friends and family. No obstacle is too high or too tough to be tackled and, again like everybody who has ridden, she has had more than her fair share of tumbles – and injuries. But she still enjoys few things more than a day in the country, riding over fields and through woodland.

Princess Michael of Kent, when she and her husband lived in Gloucestershire at Nether Lypiatt, belonged to no fewer than three hunts: the Cotswold, the Beaufort and, further afield, the Warwickshire.

She is an accomplished horsewoman and in 1983, when she was thirty-eight, she competed in the annual point-to-point organised by the Beaufort Hunt, run over a tough four-and-a-half mile course. Fifty horses started and fewer than half completed the course, of which hers was one, even though, along with several others, she ended the day by walking across the finishing line.

A year later she entered one of the hardest competitions when she competed at the Army Horse Trials at Tidworth but she did not feature among the prize winners. Princess Michael was as competitive as anyone in the royal family but, in spite of support and advice from the more experienced Princess Anne and Mark Phillips she realised her limitations and decided not to try and emulate their achievements. Her courage was never in doubt and two serious falls, which caused shoulder injuries, did not deter her from the saddle.

William and Harry were taught to ride before they were five years old and in 1995, when they were thirteen and eleven respectively, they often rode out with the Beaufort Hunt accompanied by Tiggy Legge-Bourke (now Mrs Charles Pettifer), a daughter of one of the Princess Royal's ladies-in-waiting, as they joined Prince Charles.

The young princes have tried their hands at most sports, the more competitive the better. They were introduced to polo at an early age and they both enjoyed the rough and tumble of what is supposed to be a 'non-contact' sport. But they agree that their favourite sporting activity is shooting and William in particular says he enjoys few things more than a good day's shooting accompanied by several of the Queen's gun dogs at Sandringham or Balmoral. He also likes to spend time shooting with his aunt on her estate at Gatcombe Park, where he has got to know her Labradors equally well. Among other venues he likes to visit, because he is guaranteed privacy, is the Duke of Westminster's 14,000-acre estate at Abbeystead in Lancashire (the duchess, known as Tally, is his godmother).

William is an excellent horseman and he prefers the company of larger dogs, such as black and yellow Labradors, just like his grandfather, Prince Philip. They share a belief that dogs should work and earn their keep, not just lie around doing nothing but eat and sleep. And though he has favourites among the horses he rides for pleasure, he does not regard them as pets in the real sense of the word, as he did with his ponies when he was a small boy.

The Queen has proved that enjoyment of horse riding in all its forms is something that can last a lifetime. She and Prince Philip never pushed their children into becoming competent horsemen and women, but the encouragement was there right from the beginning and their ability in the field has proved that with the right opportunities and the dedication and ambition to achieve success, anything is possible.

Similarly, Prince Charles and his siblings have not forced their own children to take up horsemanship. But it would have been strange if they had not, considering their family background in equestrian excellence.

10

Queen Victoria and Prince Albert

Queen Victoria was lucky not to be born among a bevy of lapdogs. Her mother, the Duchess of Kent, over eight months pregnant, reached Kensington Palace just days before Victoria's birth in 1819, travelling in a coach that was bursting at the seams with dogs of all shapes and sizes. The coach lurched from one pot hole to the next and a lady-in-waiting accompanying her said later she thought the duchess was going to give birth on the spot.

Queen Victoria, who in later life was not known for her gentler side, had a soft spot for animals. When she entertained guests at any of her residences, one of the highlights of the after-luncheon walks she insisted upon was a visit to the royal kennels where she knew the names and pedigrees of every dog.

Four years before she became Queen, Victoria took possession of one of her first pet dogs, Dash, by the simple expedient of taking him over from her mother. The King Charles spaniel puppy had been given to the Duchess of Kent by Sir John Conroy on 14 January 1833, in an attempt to curry favour, but the fourteen-year-old Victoria loved playing with the animal so much that her mother allowed her to keep him for herself. She even gave him Christmas presents – gingerbread decorated with holly and candles – and dressed him up in a scarlet jacket and blue trousers. When Victoria was sailing in the royal yacht, Dash was so devoted that he jumped into the sea and swam after her. He was quickly rescued before they had gone too far. And when the dog became ill, Victoria nursed him personally, keeping him with her in her room until he recovered.

When Dash died in December 1840, he was buried in the grounds at Windsor Castle (see Chapter 16).

Some years later, in 1858, the by-now Queen Victoria gave her mother a Skye terrier named Boz that remained with her until the duchess died in 1861.

It was Queen Victoria who introduced the German dachshund to Britain. The breed had a reputation for being excellent rat catchers and as Britain in the nine-teenth century was overrun with these disease-ridden rodents, a dachshund, Däckel, was accepted as a gift from the Queen's relations in Coburg and set to work at Windsor. In 1849, in the presence of the Queen, Däckel pounced and killed a giant rat in the grounds of the castle, instantly becoming a hero in Her Majesty's eyes and start-ing a dynasty of the breed that lasted for five generations. Däckel lived happily at Windsor until he died in 1860.

Another of Victoria's favourite dachshunds was Boy, who was born in the kennels at Windsor in July 1857 and died on 20 February 1863. On hearing the news Victoria recorded in her daily journal, 'gt. Sorrow to lose dear little Boy...'

Then there was Topsy, said to be a 'Scotch terrier' (there was no such breed) who was born in June 1865, along with her sister Dot. Topsy was mated with Princie in 1866 and Tinny was the result, who was also described as 'one of Queen Victoria's favourite dogs'.

Bout was a Tibetan mastiff who was a gift to Victoria from Lord Hardinge in 1847. The animal thoroughly enjoyed life in the Windsor kennels until he died in June 1856.

The Queen had a number of pugs in her collection of animals, most of whom were given to her by outsiders – in other words, commoners – which was unusual because she normally only accepted such presents from other royalty, heads of state or at least members of the British aristocracy. Two of the pugs were Venus, who provided two puppies in 1854, and Lass, who was born in 1870 and sadly lived for only three years.

In 1872 Waldman VI was brought to Windsor from Baden and immediately became Victoria's favourite (it seems that each new arrival became Her Majesty's 'favourite').

In 1884 Victoria had a rough-coated Chinese pug which sported its own business card bearing the legend 'Rat Catcher to HM Queen Victoria' – the dog had obviously taken over from Däckel.

The dogs belonging to royalty were all well used to having horses around and when Queen Victoria rode sedately on one of her favourite ponies, Sultan, in 1870 at Balmoral, she was often accompanied by Sharp, Friskie, Dacko and the late Prince Alfred's little terrier, Corran.

The Earl of Haddington gave Queen Victoria a nine-month-old white border collie named Nannie in May 1885 and she lived at Windsor for four years.

Two of Victoria's granddaughters, Princess Helena Victoria of Schleswig-Holstein and Princess Margaret of Connaught, doted on their pets and they were very much hands-on owners. In 1901 they were photographed giving one of the royal dogs his daily 'dose' of medicine. They had even taken the precaution of wrapping a clean napkin around the animal's neck to avoid any spillage – as all well-brought-up young ladies would do.

Queen Victoria's favourite painter was the artist Sir Edwin Landseer, who not only painted her and Prince Albert many times, but also their animals. He also taught the royal couple how to draw. Landseer was the highest-paid animal artist in the world in the nine-teenth century, a virtual artistic superstar, receiving on average some £200 for each royal painting. As he did over thirty for Victoria alone, it is not too difficult to see why he never complained at having to paint dogs for days on end. Three paintings of Prince Albert's favourite greyhound, Eos, were commissioned by three different artists, but only the one by Landseer was hung in a place of honour at Windsor Castle. Sir Edwin (he was knighted in 1850) also painted Victoria's pet Skye terrier, Dandie Dinmont. He and his royal patron shared a belief that animals possessed human emotions and he conveyed these attributes to his work, much to Victoria's delight.

Victoria was taken with the Dandie Dinmont terrier because of its unusual 'top-knot' of hair that is peculiar to the breed. She also liked the thought that the dog was named after a character in Sir Walter Scott's book *Guy Mannering*. The fact that the animal was also the result of cross-breeding between Scottish and Skye terriers also appealed to Her Majesty. When Landseer died in 1873 he was granted a state funeral in St Paul's Cathedral on the orders of his royal patron.

Although Queen Victoria loved all dogs, there were certain breeds that became firm favourites. Before she married Prince Albert she became very attached for a while to greyhounds. And then following the wedding in 1840, they both became enchanted with the breed and acquired several. Among them were Helios, who was born in 1864 and was one of the most handsome dogs they owned at the time, and Harlequin, born in 1863, who sported an unusual black-and-white coat, just like his namesake. Prince Albert had been given Eos, who became the most famous of all royal greyhounds, and he was so devoted to him that he recorded every event in the animal's life as if it were a significant happening, no matter how trivial. If Eos was off his food, Albert made a note in his journal; if the dog seemed particularly agile and frisky, that too was worth a mention.

In the homes of royalty, as with most of the aristocracy, their dogs were usually allowed into the dining room when they were eating. Eos would always be found by his master's feet during meal times and he would often be fed from the same fork the prince was using.

Prince Albert died prematurely in 1861 and Victoria hung Landseer's painting of the greyhound in Albert's dressing room at Buckingham Palace with orders that the room was to be kept in its original condition thereafter. Every week, servants would clean and dust the dressing room as if Albert still occupied it, taking particular care with the painting of Eos.

Giddy was another greyhound that was given to Queen Victoria by Lord Lurgan in 1873, and who, again, was most unusual in looks, having large white polka-dots all over his coat. But after Albert's death, Victoria's affection for greyhounds diminished somewhat and Giddy was banished to the kennels never to be treated as a personal pet by the Queen.

On Victoria's death in 1901, Edward VII ordered Prince Albert's room to be cleared and the painting of Eos placed in storage. Fifty years later, when her father, King George VI, died, Queen Elizabeth II did precisely the same thing with his room, keeping it just as it was when he was alive, with all his uniforms, suits, shirts and shoes in pristine condition, cleaned and pressed every week. It wasn't until her mother died in 2001 that the Queen allowed the room to be cleared.

Although Skye terriers were regarded as the favourite breed of Queen Victoria in the early days of her reign, with Scotty the first of a long line that included Islay, Dandie Dinmont, Cairnach and Boz, which came to Victoria on the death of her mother, the Duchess of Kent, she also came to own a number of much larger dogs that were gifts from abroad. There was Nelson, a Newfoundland, and Hotspur, a bloodhound, along with another new royal favourite, the collie dog, including one pure white specimen rather appropriately named Snowball. However, these larger animals were too big to be used as house pets and kept inside the royal residences so they were quickly found quarters in the royal kennels and exercised in the grounds.

The Queen was horrified at the cruelty she witnessed to cats and dogs and she personally intervened to persuade Parliament to pass several laws that would improve the lot of animals in Britain.

Victoria's concern for the welfare of all animals, including the dogs that roamed the streets of London unchecked and the thousands of cats that wandered freely throughout the country, was manifested by her interest in the early days of the Society for the Prevention of Cruelty to Animals, which was founded in 1824 and to which, in 1840, three years after she became queen, she granted the prefix 'Royal', since when the organisation has been known as the RSPCA. In 1879, her eldest son, Edward, Prince of Wales, became the society's first royal patron with the Queen herself later assuming the role. She also insisted that when a medal was being planned to mark its activities, such as acts of bravery in rescuing an animal or a particularly outstanding feat by an animal itself, a cat should be featured prominently alongside the obligatory dog. Needless to say, the organisers agreed with their royal patron.

Victoria also supported the Battersea Dogs Home, established in 1860, and it was due to her personal intervention that abandoned dogs were kept longer than the law insisted, in order to allow prospective new owners more time to make their choice. She even allowed her son, Prince Leopold, to rescue an abandoned dog called Skippy from Battersea in 1882. Skippy became a cherished royal pet, so much so that his daughter, Princess Alice of Albany, Countess of Athlone, Queen Victoria's last surviving grandchild – who died at the age of ninety-seven in Kensington Palace in 1981 – was given the pet when she begged to be allowed to look after him. This was a highly unusual act for a royal in the nineteenth century.

So, even though it was reported that the Duchess of Cornwall was the first royal to rescue a dog from Battersea, this was not true. It had been done over a hundred years earlier.

The dog licence, introduced in 1878 with the approval of Queen Victoria, cost some 7/6d per animal and it lasted more than a century before being abolished in 1988 because it cost more to administer than it raised in revenue.

Until Queen Victoria came to the throne in 1837, British people as a whole cared little for animals. The vast majority was far too busy trying to keep body and soul together to have time or the money to spend on pets.

It was Victoria who, by example, persuaded the British to adopt a kinder attitude to animals in general and dogs in particular.

Queen Victoria loved all breeds of dogs and in 1891 her collection included borzois, collies, pugs, dachshunds, poodles and terriers. Everywhere she went most of the animals went with her. To help mark Victoria's Diamond Jubilee in 1897 a troupe of poodles performed before her at Windsor Castle. She said she believed they actually enjoyed performing and that was the only reason she allowed it. Queen Victoria enjoyed showing her dogs and one of her Pomeranians, Beppo, was entered at the first Crufts Show in 1891, along with five of her other 'Poms': Fluffy, Nino, Mino, Gilda and Lulu.

Queen Victoria's pet collie Noble had only one job: to guard his royal mistress's gloves. The Queen would leave her gloves on her chair or a table and then send a servant or one of her ladies-in-waiting to fetch them. As soon as they approached the gloves Noble would growl and bare his teeth and it was a brave servant who dared to pick up the gloves after that. Victoria often deliberately sent one of the more timid servants to collect her gloves knowing what the result would be!

She had no fewer than five collies named Noble, but Noble III became the favourite. Victoria was fickle when it came to showing favouritism for certain breeds and individual animals, and during various decades in her reign she favoured many different dogs. Noble III had been given to the Queen at Balmoral on 24 May 1872 and he died, also at Balmoral, on 18 September 1887. Noble III had a daughter, grandson and great-grandchildren and he lived to see them all.

It was during the 1860s that Victoria first showed a liking for smooth-haired collies. Although as a breed they were and remain working dogs, she kept some indoors as household pets while the others were kept in the kennels.

With the increased popularity of photography in the latter part of the nineteenth century, postcards show-ing royalty were sold in their thousands. When Queen Victoria was photographed holding Sharp (1864–79), her first collie, in 1866, people clamoured for the pictures. It was these series of photographs that were credited with contributing to the growing popularity of collies in Britain. Then as now, people like to follow royalty when it comes to owning pets – or nowadays clothes. Throughout her reign, Queen Victoria owned nearly ninety collies, more than any other breed contained in the Dogs List as being the property of Her Majesty. In 1846, Victoria and Albert had so many animals that they issued a Royal List of Dogs that included twenty-three smooth-haired terriers, thirty-eight pugs and no fewer than fifty-seven Scotch terriers.

She and Albert owned no fewer than thirty-three dogs in the first ten years of their marriage alone and by the end of Victoria's reign the number had risen to eighty-eight, most of which were housed in specially built kennels at Windsor. The Queen would have liked to have them with her inside the castle, but even she agreed that this was impracticable. Still, it was not uncommon to see her walking in the grounds surrounded by a dozen or more dogs of different breeds.

In 1844 King Louis-Philippe gave Queen Victoria a French Pyrenean mountain dog, Gabbas. It was an animal with a fierce temper and attacked all and sundry including the Queen, biting her severely on the arm. Her Majesty was not used to having anything so hostile in her household and she ordered its immediate removal to the Zoological Society where it remained for the rest of its life. Gabbas was the only animal Victoria ever punished.

Lord Alfred Paget, Victoria's senior equerry, asked if he might be permitted to present Her Majesty's son the Prince of Wales with a French poodle in 1854. The Queen agreed and Bertie was thrilled with his newest acquisition, Milor.

One year later, at the conclusion of the Crimean War, a British officer brought back to England from

Sebastopol a 'captured' Russian dog named Quarry, which he presented to the Queen.

The Queen's personal doctor, Sir James Reid, on behalf of his brother, gave her a Chinese chow-chow. In return Victoria gave Sir James a white Pomeranian puppy named Vicky, with instructions that she was not to be allowed to get too fat – and she demanded regular photographs to prove the dog was being cared for according to her wishes. Sir James, who not only looked after Victoria's health, but was frequently called upon to diagnose and treat her dogs, became very attached to some of the animals, making visits to the royal kennels to chat with the keeper.

Victoria and Albert were determined that their children should become acquainted with and love animals as much as they did, so they gave each of them pets from an early age, which they had to look after on their own. Their parents said it gave them a sense of responsibility they would need in later life. The Skye terrier Corran, named for the Corran Ferry where they had bought it, was a present for Prince Alfred, 'Affie', Duke of Edinburgh, and after living at Balmoral for some years it was brought down to England where it stayed for the rest of its long life, dying in 1877 at the age of fourteen.

They also gave two of their children cats. The Princess Royal had one and so too did Prince Leopold, who named his cat Snowdrop as it was indeed snow white in colour.

If there was one common denominator that linked all Victoria's dogs it was that every one came from a long line of distinguished breeding. Her European relatives, particularly those in Germany and France, had continued the dynasties of various breeds and by careful selection and necessary 'doctoring' to eliminate any possible defects they ensured that their own dogs and those they presented to Victoria came from impeccable lines. She would never have accepted anything less.

She and Prince Albert introduced a breeding programme that was followed initially by the aristocracy and later by the middle classes – and today, of course, by animal lovers of all classes.

But not only was Victoria the recipient of magnificent dogs from abroad, she had given the offspring of many of her famous breeds to daughters, cousins and uncles who ruled Europe. So, it was Victoria who was responsible for spreading the popularity of some breeds of dogs that had hitherto been known only in Britain.

On one occasion two little Maltese dogs, Cupid and Psyche, were shipped home specifically to be presents for the Queen. Unfortunately, both animals suffered severe bouts of seasickness en route and when they finally arrived in Britain the poor animals looked so distressed that officials decreed that they were 'unsuitable' for royal eyes and so they never were presented at court.

Until the time of Queen Victoria pet dogs in Britain – and to a certain extent, other animals as well – were tethered by just a piece of string or rope, although in other countries, monarchs and princes liked to show their pets off by dressing them in elaborate clothes and diamond collars.

Queen Victoria would not allow her large dogs to wear collars but her small lapdogs were equipped with velvet collars that hadn't been seen at court for hundreds of years. Edward VII considered velvet too soft and feminine for his animals, even his pet poodle, and he had his dogs' collars made of sturdy leather, a custom that was followed by dog owners throughout Britain and which still remains to this day.

Queen Victoria found nothing strange in allowing some, but not all, of her dogs to sit in the dining room during breakfast and luncheon, but for some reason it was not considered 'proper' for them to be there at dinner.

However, one of her great favourites, the aforementioned Noble, did not join her in the dining room. Often after the meal she would take him a morsel. Her ghillie, John Brown, would stand alongside Noble, and the Queen would place a piece of cake in the animal's mouth but he would not eat it until she gave the order. Noble would then stand up on his hind legs and beg, his way of saying 'thank you'.

Most accounts of the relationship between Queen Victoria and her eldest son give the impression that there was mutual dislike and outright hostility on the part of the Queen. However, one area where they enjoyed common ground was their love of animals. Neither could see any wrong in their pets and Queen Victoria, not the most forgiving of women, found excuses for any of her animals who strayed. Just like her great-great-granddaughter.

Towards the end of her 64-year reign, when she had virtually retired to Osborne House on the Isle of Wight, she would occasionally visit Windsor and be driven in her carriage to the kennels where she would order servants to bring out her favourites one at a time so they could be handed up to her. And even in old age, Victoria remembered their names and where she had acquired them and from whom.

Queen Victoria not only had a large number of dogs, she also kept Persian cats, two of which, Flypie and White Heather, outlived her. King Edward VII and Queen Alexandra adopted both, along with the seventy dogs she left behind. She would have expected nothing less.

11

King Edward VII and Queen Alexandra

Queen Victoria was delighted that her new daughter-in-law was as fond of dogs as she was and included in the wedding presents to the couple in 1863 was a Minton dinner service decorated by Sir Edwin Landseer with pictures of their favourite dogs.

Alexandra further endeared herself to Victoria when she said, 'I like people, but I love animals.'

After their wedding, Edward and Alexandra began accumulating a menagerie of animals of many different breeds and sizes. Alexandra had two favourites: Rover, a collie, and Puggy (obviously a pug). Edward had Fozzy, a Pomeranian who was included in the entourage when the prince (as he then was) paid a visit to India in 1875. Edward also had a favourite poodle, Tom, who posed for a model sculpture that was awarded a place of honour at

Sandringham, the home bought for the Prince of Wales by Queen Victoria in 1862.

It was at Sandringham that Edward built his magnificent kennels in 1879. The kennels consisted of fifteen separate properties, each with its own exercise yard and a patch of lawn shared between every five little houses. In later years, the children of Edward and Alexandra claimed their bedrooms were much smaller and more Spartan than the kennels.

The prince and princess visited the kennels whenever they were in residence at Sandringham and it was de rigueur for all visitors to accompany them on a Sunday after luncheon, in exactly the way it had been during Queen Victoria's reign. Edward and Alexandra liked to feed the dogs themselves on these occasions and none of their guests – or members of the household who were required to be in attendance – was excused. If Edward suspected that someone was not as enthusiastic as he and his wife were, they soon became aware of his displeasure. On one occasion, an elderly gentleman, obviously feeling a little fatigued after too good a luncheon, lagged behind and was overheard muttering to himself. By the time the party returned to the main house, he found his bags had been packed and a carriage was waiting to convey him to Wolferton station. He never received another invitation to any royal home or function.

Alexandra continued to feed her animals herself well into old age, wearing a large white apron and carrying a wicker basket with white bread for the dogs – which was actually not the ideal diet for any of them. But, this being the royal way of doing things for themselves, a servant was always nearby in case there was any mess to be cleaned up.

The kennel master, a man named W. Brunsdon, was clothed in a special household livery when the royals were present. It consisted of a dark green coat and waistcoat, with gold buttons, a hat complete with gold cord and tassel, and white breeches and black, highly polished boots.

As Prince of Wales, Edward was very proud of his pet Samoyed, a gift from the German Chancellor Otto von Bismarck in 1886, so much so that the royal couple became extremely fond of the breed. Alexandra was delighted when she too received a Samoyed, Jacko, as a present from Major Frederick Jackson, who had led an expedition to Franz Josef Land in the Arctic.

Edward VII and Queen Alexandra had both been brought up with animals and they shared a passion for them throughout their lives. And as Queen Victoria had instilled in all her children a love of dogs and cats, so Edward and his wife ensured their two sons and three daughters would cherish their pets.

Three of their eldest children, Alfred Victor, Louise and George (who in 1910 became King George V), enjoyed playing with their pet black poodle who they refused to have trimmed, saying they preferred his 'shaggy' look. At the same time, Louise (who was created Princess Royal in 1905) took personal possession of a dachshund that no one else was allowed to touch, on pain of death! And this included her sister Maud.

Another daughter, Princess Victoria of Wales, who was born in 1868 and died in 1935, lived through three reigns: her grandmother, Queen Victoria; her father, Edward VII; and her brother, George V. Victoria owned a magnificent black standard poodle called Sammy with whom she would take long walks in the woods at Balmoral. She loved to have him run alongside her as she rode her upright bicycle along the paths in the garden.

Like all poodles, Sammy was a show-off and one of his favourite tricks was to balance on the backs of two wooden chairs while holding a cane in his mouth. Victoria liked Sammy to keep his head and upper torso woolly, with his long nose and rear quarters and legs shaved quite close. Sammy became a great favourite with all the royal family because of his antics and they were devastated when he tragically died in 1896 at Osborne House after accidentally eating rat poison.

Shortly after Sammy's death, Princess Victoria was given a little black terrier she named Mac. Nothing could really replace Sammy, but Mac was the next best thing and Queen Alexandra allowed the dog to accompany the royal party wherever they went, even on board the royal yacht *Victoria and Albert*. He made friends with the crew and even, surprisingly, got on with the Queen's Siamese cat, who ruled the roost and who could be a fearsome opponent, liable to attack any foe, human or animal. The cat was a hero on the yacht as he caught and killed many rats – and scratched quite a few sailors.

Alexandra was the only person he would permit to hold him and she never suffered the slightest scratch from her feline pet.

When Victoria and her mother dined on board they liked to draw sketches on the menus, depicting Mac and the cat facing each other, both wearing collars with bells on, which they had fitted to warn anyone of their presence.

Queen Alexandra loved the yacht and it was always a case of 'where I go, my pets go too'. She was often seen on board with two of her smallest dogs, a Japanese Chin and a Tibetan spaniel.

As Princess Victoria never married, she became a close companion to her mother and together they spent many hours teaching their pet dogs to perform tricks, though none achieved the expertise of Sammy the poodle.

Edward and Alexandra spared no expense on the welfare of their pets and also on buying images of them, ranging from paintings by the most celebrated artists of the day to sculptures and carvings. In 1902, the King commissioned the Russian jeweller Fabergé to make a solid silver model of his borzoi Vassilka on a beautiful marble base. Vassilka was born on 18 May 1902 and was a gift, along with another borzoi, Alix, from Tsar Alexander III and Tsarina

Maria Feodorovna, who was Queen Alexandra's sister. Vassilka was a magnificent borzoi and during his lifetime he won more than seventy-five prizes at dog shows, which delighted His Majesty, who loved owning a winner.

Another early favourite of Edward, when he became king, was an Irish terrier named Jack and the King and Queen took him with them when they paid a visit to Ireland in 1903. They were staying at Vice Regal Lodge in Dublin when Jack suddenly, without any warning, died within a day of their arrival. He was buried with due ceremony in the grounds of the lodge with this epitaph on his headstone:

HERE LIES JACK, KING EDWARD'S FAVOURITE IRISH
TERRIER WHO ONLY LIVED TWELVE HOURS AFTER
REACHING HIS NATIVE LAND. HE DIED AT VICE
REGAL LODGE ON JULY 21 1903.

Whenever Edward travelled abroad, which was frequently, one of his footmen had sole responsibility for the care of Jack's replacement, Caesar, his terrier, who became the most famous – and not always universally liked – of his pet dogs. Caesar would obey only his master and members of the royal household would often have to stand alongside Edward's desk waiting for him to sign important papers, while Caesar chewed on their trouser legs – to their natural dismay and Edward's obvious amusement. Apparently the secret was not to show any sign of discomfort. Any attempt to shake off the dog's teeth and Edward would roar with laughter and encourage him to greater efforts. If the official took absolutely no notice, both dog and his master soon tired of the incident.

Caesar was a long-haired, rough-coated, white fox terrier with black ears, who was regarded at court as a 'person of some importance'. Edward was a strict disciplinarian with all his children, but he pampered Caesar in a way that none of his sons, or his daughter, would ever experience.

Caesar had been given to the King by Lord Dudley from the kennels of the Duchess of Newcastle in 1902 and remained by his side until the day he died in 1910. Photographs of His Majesty's state funeral procession appeared in every newspaper of the day showing Caesar trotting faithfully behind the carriage bearing the royal coffin. The King also commissioned Fabergé to create a likeness of his little rough-haired terrier and another of Queen Alexandra's pet standard poodle.

His Majesty suffered a serious illness in 1902 and to aid his recovery it was decided that he would take a cruise on board the *Victoria and Albert*. His personal physician accompanied him to supervise his convalescence and most afternoons, when the King was resting in his suite, the doctor insisted that no one, including the Queen, should disturb him. There were no exceptions – apart from Caesar, to whom no rules applied. He was never banned from his master's presence and later, even the doctor admitted, albeit grudgingly, that perhaps the animal had contributed to the King's rapid recovery.

Unlike most members of the royal family, who objected – they still do – if anyone else petted or even fed the dogs, Edward loved it when his friends showed their affection for Caesar, which some of them did by feeding him titbits from their own plates at meal times.

One exception was Violet, the daughter of Edward's mistress of long standing, Alice Keppel (the great-grandmother of the present Duchess of Cornwall), who detested the animal, saying he 'stank to high Heaven'. And she particularly hated it when Edward plonked Caesar on her lap when they were out driving. He realised her antipathy to the dog but it amused him to force Violet to accept him on behalf of her mother – because there was no question of a refusal.

Caesar's popularity with the British public was exemplified when, in 1910, he 'wrote' a book called *Where's Master?* which sold over 100,000 copies. The book was first published on 13 June 1910 and by 3 September that year it had entered its tenth reprint, becoming its publisher's outstanding commercial success of the year.

The book is a brilliant account of life at court as seen through the eyes of Caesar and tells of how the little dog misses his master, without knowing exactly where he has gone or why.

On the opening page, Caesar says, 'I've been hunting for him high and low for days. I can't find Master anywhere, and I'm so lonely … I want to feel his warm hand catch hold of my nose and waggle my head slowly to and fro.' He goes on to say he will not let anyone else do that for him because only Master knows how to do it properly. Then he mentions how the others in the Palace are trying to comfort him.

> They have just brought me my dinner. They say She [Queen Alexandra] ordered it specially for me … I thought I'd try a mouthful to please Her. But it tasted bitter like medicine. I want a bone from Master's plate. I never worry him when he's at table, but he knows I'm always there beside the right leg of his chair. And Master never forgets his little dog, however many important people he may have to feed.

Caesar gives a canine insight into the events leading up to Edward VII's death and how confused he was when he couldn't join his master in his bedroom. He trots from room to room in Buckingham Palace, mentioning that he has to be very careful when walking in the throne room because it has a very slippery floor; he has to walk on the tips of his nails so he won't leave a scratch. He says he knows someone is inside one of the rooms because he has heard voices 'just like those I've listened to while Master was in church and I was outside waiting for him … Master says I've never been quite good enough to take inside church – though I've been almost everywhere else with him.' Which was quite true. The King had Caesar alongside wherever he was; working, playing, at home or abroad. On one of their trips overseas, Caesar had growled at a French poodle and His Majesty had said that he was a typical Englishman who couldn't meet a foreigner without growling and strutting about as if the whole world had been created for him. Edward was, of course, describing himself and his attitude to anyone who did not have the good fortune to be born English. Sunday service was the only occasion when the little companion and his master were separated.

Just two weeks before Edward died, the family had been staying at Sandringham and Edward was plainly unwell, though he refused to admit it, saying he was merely overtired. But he never missed church. It was expected of him and he did not neglect his duty. That final Sunday afternoon at Sandringham Edward took Caesar and Daisy, one of his other dogs, for a long walk in the park. It was almost as if His Majesty knew this might be his last visit to the home he loved and he asked his agent to show him all the preparations for the coming year, as Caesar recalled: 'Show me everything, and arrange everything for the year, so that She may find everything ready when She comes down.'

Caesar then revealed that he had had an animal's premonition, without realising what it was, of what was shortly to happen to his master:

I always sleep in Master's bedroom … just as I was getting off to sleep in the early morning, I started up and every hair on my back stood on end, for in the corner of the room I saw a strange dark shadow… 'Lie still, Caesar,' said the voice from the bed, 'I've got a bit of a cough, old man, and that's what disturbed you.'

But Master didn't see what I saw … and I waited and watched the shadow.

In the royal train travelling back from Wolferton to London the following day, Caesar sat on his master's lap as he usually did. He noticed that the King was coughing very badly, so much so that Edward put Caesar aside, telling him that his cough would disturb him and he wanted his pet to be comfortable. But Caesar knew his place was with master and he refused to budge; for the first time he had disobeyed a royal order. But the King was too weak to argue and allowed Caesar to remain on his knees for the entire journey.

At Buckingham Palace the next day Caesar saw lots of strange people and they wouldn't let him into his master's room, which was unusual. He barked outside until he heard master say,

'Let Caesar come in at once' … There were three or four black-coated men around him, and the room smelt

so funny. She was there, standing beside the chair…
'Hush, little man,' said She, 'Master's not at all well.'

It was near the end for Edward and Caesar stayed at his feet for hours, until someone came and carried him out of the room.

> Master's dead. Oh, yes, I know what that means. I know so well that I wish, I wish so much, that I could die too. She has told me, Master's dead. I shall never see him or feel him again. And She is sorrowing too … only more – so much more because She is Human, and Humans have bigger hearts … I only have a tiny heart, but it was full of love for dear Master.

When Edward died, Caesar pined for days for his master, refusing to budge from outside his bedroom where he thought Edward still lay. Eventually it was Alexandra who coaxed him into her own boudoir, where she lavished attention on him until the day of the funeral, at which Caesar stole the show.

In his book Caesar tells of the moment when Queen Alexandra agrees that he can march in the funeral procession, even though little dogs never march in processions.

She says I can go if I am very good and follow close behind Master, and walk very slowly, and never move from the centre of the road … I wonder if Master knows, and is pleased that, after all, his little dog is going with him on his last journey.

The ending of Caesar's little book is heart-rending and poignant: 'They say I can't follow Master any further. They say there are no little dogs where Master has gone. But I know better.'

It was a fitting end to a companionship that had been enjoyed for twelve years.

Queen Alexandra, to whom none of her animals could do any wrong, appalled some of her guests – but of course, they did not show it – by allowing a Pekingese to walk on the dinner table when they were eating and also to eat off the plates. It was also alleged that her animals were fed far better than her servants – and some royal servants complained – out of hearing of course – that the dogs were also far better housed, particularly in the kennels.

Alix, Queen Alexandra's borzoi, was kept in absolute luxury. It enjoyed the freedom of the house, without being fully house trained, and servants would follow it around waiting to clean up any mess it might leave, which it frequently did. If it had remained in Russia, where the breed was favoured by the Tsar, it would have been destroyed as all so-called 'aristocratic' animals were by the Bolsheviks in 1918, following the revolution. Borzois, bloodhounds, poodles and any breed of lapdog were all sought out by the revolutionaries and deliberately hanged or shot, just as anything that was associated with the upper classes was destroyed or vandalised. Even pet cats and rabbits belonging to the children of the aristocracy were destroyed in a frenzy of anti-Tsarist revenge.

It was as Princess of Wales that Alexandra became patron of the Ladies Kennel Association in 1894 and this was no mere 'letter-head' appointment. She took her responsibilities seriously and became involved in every aspect of the association's activities. She was particularly keen on promoting the interests of its lady artist members and two of them received commissions to paint Edward's and Alexandra's pets at Buckingham

Palace – under the strict personal supervision of Alexandra, who insisted on being present at all times.

Edward VII received a Siberian sheepdog named Luska in 1908 and when the dog fell ill and refused to eat his usual diet of meat, Alexandra took control of his treatment and personally fed him fish and rice, which she had been told was excellent food for sick animals. Luska recovered.

It was Edward VII who insisted that his spaniels should be categorised as King Charles spaniels, overruling the Kennel Club, who preferred to call them English toy spaniels. English monarchs had unofficially called their spaniels 'King Charles' for centuries, since they were first associated with King Charles II (1660–85), but the breed did not receive its official recognition until Edward VII made his ruling in 1902. And the Cavalier King Charles did not become an official breed until as late as 1945, at the end of the Second World War.

A King Charles spaniel was involved in the tragic events following the overthrow of the Russian tsar and his family in 1918. Grand Duchess Anastasia Nikolaevna of Russia owned one of the breed as her favourite pet and when the Tsar and his entire family were shot by the Bolsheviks on 17 July 1918, the corpse of a King Charles spaniel was also found on the site where the bodies of the Tsar, his wife and their children had been burnt.

King Edward VII was a man who had, in his early life, earned a reputation for fast living, gambling, mixing with unsuitable companions and failing to face up to his responsibilities. As monarch, he quickly became one of the most popular sovereigns Britain had known – even if he did retain his fondness for the ladies. But one thing both he and Queen Alexandra should be remembered for is their concern for the welfare of all animals; not only their own, but everyone else's. If that is the major part of their legacy, it is no small inheritance to pass on to their successors.

12

King George V and Queen Mary

In 1893, the second son of the Prince of Wales (later King Edward VII), Prince George, married Princess Mary of Teck, known as May. On his marriage, Queen Victoria made George Duke of York and the new duke and duchess, like those before them, immediately began collecting a menagerie ranging from the mandatory dogs and cats to birds. It was a collection that was to last throughout both their lives, first as duke and duchess and then as king and queen. They both gave the impression to outsiders that they were unfeeling and cold, but where their animals were concerned nothing could have been further from the truth. They loved all their pets to distraction and suffered sheer misery when one of them was hurt or even worse when it died.

Their first dog was Heather, a handsome collie who lived with them at their London home, York House, part of St James's Palace, where today the Princess Royal has an apartment. Heather, who lived to the age of eleven, dying in 1904, was the first of five dogs that were kept as personal pets and it was unusual to find such a large dog inside the house.

Next to arrive was a pug in 1895 and his place in his master's affections was illustrated when the little dog was photographed being held wrapped in one of his owner's coats and even a headscarf to protect him from the cold.

In 1901, on the death of Queen Victoria, George's father became king and he in turn relinquished the title of Duke of York, being elevated to the senior rank of Prince of Wales.

In the summer months, when the royal family moved en masse to Scotland, the Prince and Princess of Wales took up residence in Abergeldie Castle, which had been owned by the Gordon family for over five hundred years but had been leased by the royal family since 1848 (until 1970). The castle is very near Balmoral. It was there that the prince enjoyed walking for hours, alone apart from the company of his terrier Happy. The dog became a celebrity in its own right, like Caesar even publishing a book 'written' by itself in April 1911 under the title *If I Were King George*. It became an instant best seller. Priced at 1/- (5p) in hardback, or 2/- (10p) in cloth, it was a companion piece to *Where's Master?* 'written' by Caesar and was an equal success. The book very cleverly told the story of what it was like for the new monarch (George V succeeded his father when he died in 1910) – and his dog – to take over from the extremely popular Edward VII and his pet. It began by saying that Caesar should accept that Happy was now the King's dog and Buckingham Palace was now his domain. Happy tells of the day when his master, King George V, comforted Caesar after Happy had tried to show him who was boss and they had had an argument. 'As I passed through the door I heard King George say: "Here, Caesar! Poor old boy. Don't take any notice. He doesn't understand."'

Happy was angry with his master and with Caesar, who he blamed for the row, but he was pleased when the King made friends once again. 'Happy', he said very quietly, and his voice was curious as if he was speaking to himself,

the King cannot be like other men, and I suppose they'll expect something different from the King's dog, too. I'm beginning to understand what it means to be King, and you've got to understand too, little man ... Go and talk to Caesar. His master understood better than anyone else, and he had no secrets from his little dog.

Happy goes on to explain, through his eyes, how his master has to cope with 'this wretched business of State' and how it interferes with their games. The book also goes into some detail about the concerns of certain people about cruelty to animals and birds when Happy meets a little bird (who he is surprised to find speaks fluent dog) and who begs him to intervene with Queen Mary, who wears bird feathers in her hats.

> ...if she can spare one moment in those busy times to give a thought to those most humble subjects of hers in far-off lands, whose beautiful white plumage is so cruelly torn off at the time when they need it most, just to adorn humans' heads and hats ... if Queen Mary only said the word – she's a mother, you know, and will understand.

The little bird then adds a plea to sportsmen to shoot straight: 'We know we're made to be shot at. If only we might die quickly we should be so grateful.'

The book drew attention to a number of concerns, all of which were seen through the eyes of Happy and Caesar – and the little bird in the garden at Buckingham Palace. And Caesar told Happy how he should behave now that he was the King's dog and also that he should forgive human beings as 'they don't begin to understand animals, let alone each other'.

Happy's insight into the new king's behaviour portrayed His Majesty as someone who was learning his trade, trying to look interested even when he was bored stiff.

One of the most fascinating aspects of *If I Were King George* is when the old Caesar is telling the young Happy how his master, King Edward VII, got his name as the Peacemaker, and how the relationship between England and France became known as the Entente Cordiale. Edward had said to Caesar one evening, 'A cordial understanding is worth all the treaties in the world, isn't it?' Then he repeated something in French that the little dogs had heard before but didn't understand, '*Tout comprendre, c'est tout pardoner* – To understand all, is to forgive all.'

This little book – it is only fifty-five pages long – is not a children's book, though it is written in a manner that young readers would appreciate. Rather it is a clever, subtle essay into the way an animal feels about his master. It also gives a unique glimpse of life behind Palace curtains, examining the monarchical and political issues of the day.

Caesar and Happy discuss why Edward VII is no longer with them and neither understands the reason why one of them has been left alone and had his place usurped by a younger little dog.

They even ask each other if 'She' (the way they always referred to Queen Alexandra) would know why Edward is no longer with them and why his son George is now the king, with Happy occupying the privileged position as the king's dog, previously held by Caesar. But they are reluctant to ask the queen. 'There must be Someone somewhere, Who knows and understands everything, and I am sure He has told Her and explained. But She can't tell me, although She's tried ... I'd so gladly die tomorrow if only I could understand.' The ending of the book is quite optimistic as the crown passes from father to son, with the new king learning the ropes of monarchy. Happy says if he were king he would make everyone understand, but wise old Caesar says you cannot do it simply by making them understand. They have to be persuaded slowly. The final exchange between the two dogs reassures Happy when he asks Caesar if King George will know the way forward. 'Of course,' says Caesar, 'Master will have told him. He's Master's son, you see.'

Happy, who was the first of four terriers the King would own, died in 1913.

Some years later, His Majesty owned another pet terrier who he named Jack, as a compliment to his late father's favourite terrier of the same name.

The two-year-old Princess Elizabeth (now Queen Elizabeth II) was greatly loved by her grandparents and when they took her to Balmoral in the summer of 1928, she was introduced to Snip, who had by now become the King's pet cairn terrier – and also to Charlotte, the parrot, of whom Snip was always very wary. Snip was particularly loved because he had been given to the King by his beloved daughter, Princess Mary, later the Princess Royal.

Like most dogs, Snip loved the water and his royal master would often wade through Loch Muick followed closely by Snip, swimming hard trying to keep up.

George V had enormous affection for cairn terriers and his last dog was naturally another of the same breed. Called Bob, the animal outlived the king by twelve years, dying in September 1938.

His collar, which was designed by His Majesty, bore the words 'I BELONG TO THE KING' and it is preserved to this day at Windsor Castle.

George V loved his working dogs as much as he did the little pet breeds, and he took an active interest in them all, especially the distinctive Clumber spaniels that were housed in the Wolferton kennels near Sandringham.

In Britain it was not until George V came to the throne that royal dog owners accepted the advice of canine experts regarding the diet of their pets. Before then, dogs were given any scraps that were left if they were working dogs or fancy titbits from the royal table if they were lapdogs, no matter how unsuitable the food might be. It was a matter of 'if it's good enough for me, it's good enough for them'.

Spaniels, for example, should be fed only the best of British fare: minced, lean, undercooked beef, mixed with brown bread cut into tiny squares, with green vegetables two or three times a week and the occasional dessert of rice pudding.

Queen Mary's Pekes were fed fish, rice and liver and the occasional pick-me-up dose of Virol.

But once George V had died, royal dogs were given a more balanced diet – apart from those owned by Queen Mary, who insisted she knew better than the experts. And in fact, her animals did all live to a ripe old age.

One of King George V's animals, a great favourite, if not exactly a pet, was involved in one of the most bizarre and tragic events of the early part of the twentieth century. Anmer, the King's racehorse, ridden by Herbert Jones, was an entry in the Derby at Epsom in 1913, when a Suffragette, Emily Davison, ducked under the rails and walked out onto the track, in an attempt to attract publicity to the cause of women's voting rights. It has never been agreed whether she did intend to kill herself or merely to attach a notice proclaiming women's rights to the horse's saddle. However, she was hit by the King's oncoming horse and later died of her injuries; fortunately neither Anmer nor the jockey were hurt. However, Herbert Jones never recovered from the shock and it is said he was haunted by the image of what had happened for the rest of his life.

Charlotte, the pink-grey parrot gifted to the King by his adored sister Princess Victoria when he was just eleven years old, remained with him until the day he died in 1935. Charlotte was given the freedom of any room His Majesty was in and guests who were being entertained to luncheon or dinner had to suffer the fact that Charlotte would fly freely around the room and, just as freely, relieve herself all over the place. Queen Mary loathed the bird and the King used to quietly move the condiments around the dining table in an effort to disguise the droppings. It didn't always work and the staff had the unpleasant task of cleaning up after every meal.

Visitors to Buckingham Palace on official business often found His Majesty working diligently on his 'Red Boxes' with Charlotte perched happily on his shoulder.

When George V died, his body was carried in the royal train from Norfolk to London for the lying-in-state in Westminster Hall. On his prior instructions, Charlotte was brought along in the train – this time in her cage – along with Queen Mary, who still despised the bird.

The King was buried in St George's Chapel at Windsor Castle and the Royal Archives at Windsor record that Charlotte was then returned to Sandringham where she lived under the protection of the housekeeper – with strict instructions to keep her away from Queen Mary at all times.

13

The Duke and Duchess of Windsor

In 1896, when he was barely two years old, Prince Edward of York (later the Duke of Windsor) became attached to Sammy (his aunt's poodle) who quickly became a favourite. They adored each other and Edward was distraught when Sammy died after accidentally eating rat poison that had been laid down to kill the vermin that plagued even royal houses in the nineteenth century.

No one ever doubted that Edward, even as a child, loved dogs, but his feelings towards other animals were not so affectionate, as an incident when he was just eight years old proves. Together with his sister, Princess Mary, later the Princess Royal, he was playing in the garden of a house called Orchard Lea, near Windsor Castle. It was later discovered that all the family's baby ducks had been killed and laid out in a row near the lake.

He never admitted the offence, and both he and Mary refused to deny they were the culprits when charged. It was an act so violent and barbaric that the young prince was banned from that particular house. Not that he gave the slightest indication that he was worried, but he would have been if the incident had been reported to his father, the Duke of York (later King George V), who was a fierce disciplinarian whose punishments were greatly feared by all his children.

In 1935, when the future Edward VIII was still Prince of Wales, he gave Wallis Simpson, the woman who would be the cause of a constitutional crisis in Britain, a cairn terrier named Slipper, who rapidly became the favourite pet of both of them.

Slipper was of the breed that originated in Scotland when they were first known as short-haired Skye terriers; the name was changed to cairn only in 1909. It is claimed that the name derives from the fact that the terriers are able to squeeze into the piles of stones in Scotland known as cairns, when they chase rabbits.

Since the days when he first became king, Edward urged his first pet cairn terrier Cora (the predecessor to Slipper) to sleep on his bed. In admitting that the dog had slept on or near his bed, Edward was following the custom of his parents, grandparents and his great-grandmother, Queen Victoria, who had each not only allowed but welcomed the presence of their pets in their bedroom. And when she became too old to jump up on the bed he had a special set of steps built to help her. He also ordered a set of spectacles because she apparently suffered from sickness when flying with him and the glasses helped. Whether they did or not, the optician who supplied the spectacles was, no doubt, delighted with the unusual – and expensive – order.

Money was no object to Edward and Wallis where their pets were concerned.

As well as the spectacles made for Cora, the couple had a pair of mink-lined ear muffs designed for the animal, who was apparently also disturbed by aircraft noise. How they managed to get them to stay on the dog's head is anyone's guess.

During the abdication crisis of 1936, King Edward VIII was parted for several weeks from his future wife, Wallis, who had left Britain to stay in France until he was able to join her.

In his memoirs, Edward wrote:

In the bitter days that followed I was to be grateful for his [Slipper's] companionship. He followed me around The Fort [Belvedere, his private country home on the edge of Windsor Great Park]; he slept by my bed; he was mute witness of my meetings with the Prime Minister ... Except for Slipper, the living bonds between us had momentarily parted.

The King's last hours as sovereign and emperor were marked by his preparations to leave Britain for good. As he waited to make his farewell abdication speech, to be broadcast to the Empire, he found the little dog Slipper constantly at his heels (Cora had already been sent abroad.)

The pet must have sensed that something was wrong when a small group of the King's aides gathered in the hall of The Fort to say their goodbyes to their sovereign.

Slipper became agitated and Edward, trying to reassure him that he was not going to be left behind, patted him and said, 'Of course you are coming with me, Slipper, but you cannot come to this family dinner,' referring to the farewell meal he was attending that evening at Royal Lodge with his mother, Queen Mary, his sister, the Princess Royal, and his three brothers, Bertie, who became King George VI the next day, Henry, Duke of Gloucester and George, Duke of Kent.

As the Duke of Windsor recalled in his memoirs, he

then turned to Walter Monckton (his closest adviser and former attorney general when he was Prince of Wales) and said, 'Be sure to bring Slipper with you in the car when you come to fetch me for the broadcast.'

Monckton was as good as his word and when he arrived to accompany the King to Windsor Castle where he was to make the historic broadcast, His Majesty found Slipper waiting for him sitting in the car, obviously bewildered at finding himself out at night, which was a departure from his normal routine. Both dog and master were equally comforted by the other's presence.

Shortly afterwards, the by-now Duke of Windsor tucked Slipper under his arm for safety as he walked up the gangway of HMS *Fury*, the Royal Navy destroyer that sailed from Portsmouth to take them both (the duke and his little dog) into permanent exile.

For all his faults, the Duke of Windsor would not have even considered leaving Slipper behind. Previously, as Prince of Wales, he and Wallis Simpson travelled with Slipper in the summer of 1935. They always referred to the dog as 'Ours' not 'Yours' or 'Mine'.

Edward was another who abused the quarantine laws when he became king and also after the abdication when he no longer had the protection of royal immunity. Mrs Simpson, when she became Duchess of Windsor, said, 'Laws only apply to others.' In her memoirs, Wallis Simpson explained how she had fled to France to escape the row caused by their affair.

> I decided that because of the uncertainties ahead, I could not take with me the little cairn, Slipper, whom David had given me at the beginning of our friend-ship [two years earlier] and whom I had come to love dearly … One evening he [David] telephoned to say he was sending back to me my dog, Slipper, to be a companion on my walks.

When Slipper was delivered two days later Mrs Simpson records, 'The dog's joyous recognition was like a signal to me that … David had sent part of himself.'

This version contradicts the account in the Duke of Windsor's memoirs where he states that Slipper stayed with him until the day of the abdication. But what is true is that when the couple had retired to live in France, Wallis was walking on a golf course some months later, with Slipper tagging along behind, when he disappeared into the bushes, chasing rabbits. She looked everywhere for him and finally saw what she thought was a piece of cloth lying on the grass. It turned out it was Slipper, who had been bitten by a viper and was now in agony. He died that same evening in a veterinary clinic in Tours. After the dog's funeral at Candé on 6 April 1937, the duke commissioned a diamond-encrusted slipper embedded in a medallion, which was then given a place of honour in their future home in the Bois de Boulogne in Paris.

It was during the 1950s that the Duke and Duchess of Windsor started their strain of pugs, eventually owning no fewer than nine of the breed. It is alleged that it was the duchess who persuaded the duke to change his affiliation from the cairn terriers he had earlier preferred because of her animosity towards Queen Elizabeth (later the Queen Mother). Elizabeth was believed to dislike pugs and Wallis bought the animals as an act of open defiance to her sister-in-law (even though Elizabeth never acknowledged her as such). But the duke later admitted that his preference for the breed was because of their compact, well-proportioned bodies, easily identifiable, flat, wrinkled faces and tightly curled tails. He said they reminded him of some of his relations but declined to say which ones.

They say vengeance is a dish best eaten cold and

Wallis waited nearly twenty years to get her own back on the woman who, as queen consort, she believed had been the reason why she (Wallis) had been refused the style of Her Royal Highness normally accorded to the wife of a royal prince. By this time the Queen Mother had become her long-time enemy. In 1955, the Queen Mother's younger daughter, Princess Margaret, was involved in a highly publicised love affair with a crown equerry, Group Captain Peter Townsend, a divorced RAF officer. In a childish gesture that was plainly intended to infuriate the Queen Mother – and humiliate the rest of the royal family – Wallis announced that she was naming one of her pugs Peter Townsend. There was no official reaction from Buckingham Palace or Clarence House but privately it was said that the arrow had struck home and the Queen Mother – and Princess Margaret – were furious.

The Duke of Windsor was a surprisingly accomplished and enthusiastic worker of needlepoint from an early age, and he personally embroidered pictures of his pug pets on to expensive cushions, which were scattered around his various houses.

The duchess used her husband's valet, Sidney Johnson,

who went on to manage the household in their mansion in the Bois de Boulogne in Paris, to look after her pugs, a duty he was said to have accepted with some reluctance.

The Duke and Duchess of Windsor lavished beauty treatment on their pugs, often sending them to pets' beauty parlours in France where they would spend the day before being feted as guest of honour at dog parties. Their leads were woven from silver and gold thread, and the duke and duchess would dress their four favourite pugs, Disraeli, Trooper, Imp and Davy Crockett, in identical wing collars and bow ties, for their celebrated dinner parties to which the dogs were always invited, as well as the human guests – some of whom were not always as appreciative of the animals as their royal hosts.

The Duke of Windsor was accused of being shallow and uncaring, and a man who had neglected his duty to his country. But there is no doubt that his feelings for his animals – his pet dogs in particular – were genuine. Perhaps he and his wife substituted the dogs for the children they never had. They certainly lavished attention and love in equal measure on each of their pets and were heartbroken when one of them died.

14

Royal Working Dogs

Among the least known and perhaps most exclusive breeds of dog the royal family has owned is the Clumber spaniel. First established at Sandringham by Prince Albert in the nineteenth century, the Clumber spaniel never achieved the popularity of other royal dogs such as the cocker spaniels, corgis and Labradors, which is a pity because they are arguably the most loyal and friendly of all.

Prince Albert had been given a pair of Clumber spaniels by the Duke of Newcastle. The name 'Clumber' comes from the Nottinghamshire estate of the Duke of Newcastle and Prince Albert was so impressed by the quality of his gift that he began a breeding programme that was very successful for many years.

Numerically they are a small breed with registrations rarely rising above 200 puppies a year. In fact, in 2003 the Kennel Club identified the Clumber spaniel as a vulnerable British breed.

Used mainly as a gun dog that specialises in hunting in heavy cover, the Clumber is by far the largest and heaviest of all spaniels, standing between 17 and 20 inches; its heavy bone structure gives it an average weight of 85 pounds.

They are said to be gentle, loyal and affectionate, yet they seem to have a permanently sad and mournful expression on their faces.

They are ideal for hunting in wet gorse or woodland as their coats are completely weather resistant.

At Sandringham they came into their own during the partridge-shooting season, and at Balmoral they were also in their element on the 'Glorious 12th' when the grouse season begins.

The last British monarch to breed Clumbers was George V, who loved the animals. Unfortunately, when he died in 1936, his heir, Edward VIII, took little interest in the breed – or for that matter the kennels, and neither King George VI nor his daughter, our present Queen, saw fit to revive royal involvement with Clumber spaniels.

When Edward VIII came to the throne (for just eleven months) in 1936, he set out on a programme of cost cutting; among the first to suffer was the Clumber kennels at Sandringham. When he discovered how much they cost to maintain, he was furious and ordered their destruction and the dispersal of the animals. In his memoirs he recalled that

> my enquiring gaze fell upon the Sandringham accounts ... where no expense had been spared to maintain Sandringham as a model property: but that praise-worthy reputation had been preserved only by dipping into the Privy Purse with a prodigality that was the wonder of my father's neighbours. And game birds for the King and his guests to shoot were still being raised on a scale that could hardly have been surpassed in the country.

The fact that the Clumber kennels had been the favourites of both his father, George V, and his grandfather, Edward VII, cut no ice with him. The high reputation the kennels enjoyed throughout the world also failed to impress him.

George V had won first prize at Crufts in 1932 and

again in 1934 with his Clumber Sandringham Spark. As it happened, the kennel master at Sandringham, Alfred Higgs, delayed the destruction of the kennels (without telling the King) and instead merely sold the dogs – for very substantial sums, as everyone wanted a dog with such impressive credentials and royal provenance – so the huge savings ordered by the King were made without having to physically destroy the kennels.

As soon as Bertie replaced his brother Edward as sovereign, becoming King George VI and the last emperor, His Majesty restocked the kennels at Sandringham with just half a dozen yellow Labradors (some people call them golden Labradors, but there is no such breed, they are yellow), from which has sprung the present healthy strain of gun dogs which is so successful in trials all over the country. They are by far the most popular of the retrievers and because of their fondness for water they are used, as the name implies, for retrieving game from lakes and rivers. They also excel as both working dogs and household pets.

These yellow Labradors supplemented the black Labradors that had been at Sandringham since they were introduced by Queen Alexandra in 1911, with the name Wolferton attached to each animal, Wolferton being not only the name of the nearby village but, more importantly, the tiny railway station, just two miles from Sandringham, that was used by generations of royalty when arriving at and departing from the estate. The last royal train departed from Wolferton in 1966 and the station was closed in 1969, but long before that, King George V, who had allowed the Wolferton name to remain affixed to the breed in deference to his mother, changed it to Sandringham on her death in 1925, and it has remained so ever since.

Sixteen years after Elizabeth II came to the throne, the kennels at Sandringham, which until then had been rather large brick structures, were replaced by smaller wooden kennels that could house in comfort nearly fifty dogs. The Queen acted on the recommendation of the then kennel master, proving that she is not above accepting advice from her servants when she recognises that they have more experience than her.

Much of the Queen's success with gun dogs is due to the expertise of her former, long-time gun dog handler,

Bill Meldrum, who first joined Her Majesty's staff in 1963 and worked non-stop until he retired in 2000.

When they first met, the Queen told Bill that she was keen to own a field trials champion and, from the thirty-five or so Labradors she kept at Sandringham, he produced no fewer than five champions during his long career.

He was also instrumental in instructing Her Majesty in the craft of 'handling' and he claimed that she was among the best he had ever seen. He added that she could control her personal favourite black Labrador, Sherry, from a distance of 800 yards without once uttering a spoken word. It was all done with whistles and hand signals.

Bill Meldrum says that gun dog trials are the ultimate test for dog and handler and Her Majesty never asked for, nor was she ever given, the slightest help on the competition field because of who she is. In field trials rank and status has little meaning; it is the quality of the dog and the expertise of the handler that impress the judges, nothing more. And, indeed, if the Queen had thought for one moment that she was being given an unfair advantage over her fellow competitors, she would have retired from the field. All she wanted was a level playing field; no more, no less. And that is exactly what she received. It is worth noting that since Mr Meldrum retired, the Queen has not entered a single trial; when he retired, so did she, such was her reliance on his guidance.

Today the number of Labradors has been reduced to around twenty and the Queen no longer sells any of their puppies. Previously, if a bitch gave birth to a litter of eight, two would be retained at Sandringham for training or further breeding and six would be sold, but only to good homes once the Queen and Mr Meldrum were satisfied that the buyer wanted the dogs for their working qualities only and not simply because of their royal provenance, which obviously attracted a number of well-off social climbers. There have always been people who would love to be able to claim a special relationship with royalty by being able to say that their pet dog came from the royal kennels at Sandringham, and perhaps hinting that they had been given it by the Queen herself.

The relationship between the Queen and her gun dogs is very different from the one that she enjoys with her corgis.

The Labradors and cocker spaniels are very much

working dogs who earn their keep, while the corgis are Her Majesty's constant companions in town and country. The only time she is separated from them is when she travels abroad. They are then housed with a 'corgi sitter' in a 'grace and favour' home on the Windsor Castle estate.

Prince Philip's preference is for the gun dogs who accompany him when he is shooting. Just like the Queen, he too likes to name his own dogs, some of which have been called after popular makes of motor car – all British: Austin, Rover but not so far a Rolls-Royce. He has also called the occasional dog after a hat, such as Trilby, and though there was once a Bowler no one has heard him shout out for 'Top Hat'. Prince Philip has a working dog named Minx, after the Hillman car that bore the same name, while her son is called Maestro, again after a motor car, this time a now defunct Austin.

The cocker spaniels were first involved in hunting wood-cock and it is from this that the name 'cocker' is said to originate. Flash, a favourite cocker spaniel, was given to the Queen when he was just six weeks old and he is said to love a cuddle in the morning. He doesn't get one from the Queen but one of the stable lasses can't resist picking him up before taking him off to work. Two of the other cocker spaniels' names show the Queen's sense of humour. They are Oxo and Bisto, obviously so named because of their colouring. Both are very frisky and they cannot be worked on the same day as they are apt to cause minor chaos.

The earliest record of springer spaniels to be bred in England belongs to the Duke of Norfolk, the country's premier Catholic peer, who can trace ancestry of his dogs back to the reign of James II in the seventeenth century. James accepted gifts of spaniels from the duke because, as a fellow Roman Catholic, he wanted dogs that sprang from a predominantly Catholic home; presumably he imagined the animals shared their master's faith! So the breed became a royal favourite – and it didn't do Norfolk any harm either.

The kennels at Sandringham have produced five field-trial champions during the Queen's reign and today they house around twenty-two fully grown dogs. They are trained for use by the royal family when they shoot and, when the family is not in residence, the gamekeepers use them as working dogs on the estate.

At Sandringham, where all her gun dogs are housed, the Queen loves to work them herself whenever it is possible, and experts have claimed she appears to be as one with them and in turn they seem to know how much she appreciates their efforts when they do something right. But, she is also a hard taskmaster and is not easily pleased.

When she was younger, the Queen would occasionally act as a judge at Kennel Club Retriever Trials at Sandringham. These were always held on private land because if it became known that she was making an appearance at a public venue the security problems would have been enough to cause the police nightmares.

In 1984, the Queen acted as judge at the Kennel Club's Two-Day Retriever Trials, which were held on the Sandringham estate that year. The Kennel Club had been invited by the Queen to hold their event on her land and they, in turn, returned the compliment by asking her to become a judge. This had nothing to do with the fact that she was the sovereign, which did of course add great prestige to the trials, but because her reputation as a gun dog handler over many years had prompted the invitation. Experts had compared her favourably with many professionals in the craft.

The Queen was at first reluctant, but after careful consideration she accepted with one proviso: there was to be no advance publicity. The first the observers knew of Her Majesty's presence and her role was when they saw her name on the meeting card for the day. And workers on the royal estate and neighbouring farms all guaranteed the discretion Her Majesty needed to do the job on this occasion.

Somewhat surprisingly, the Queen once confided to a lady-in-waiting that she was nervous standing and judging in front of all those highly experienced gun dog handlers, every one of them a severe critic. Considering that she had spent and continues to spend her life in the public eye, when not one person has ever seen the slightest hint of nerves, it might have been expected that she would regard simply being a judge at a trials as little more than a relaxation. Anyway, the Queen has not been a judge for many years and these days she is content to be just another spectator – and one with an expert eye earned through many years of field experience.

Like every other competitor, the Queen has always liked to win. But she is a true adherent to the Olympic ideal: it is the taking part that matters, not only the winning. She treats victory and defeat with equanimity, whether it is a cause for jubilation or disappointment. She learned this lesson from her mother, who when one of her horses failed to win always simply remarked, 'That's racing.'

The gun dogs have an uncanny instinct of knowing when the Queen or the Duke of Edinburgh is near. They start barking and acting wildly. The staff say they have no idea how they know but long before the royal couple are anywhere near the kennels, the dogs react.

One of Her Majesty's gun dogs, Gem, was brought to Sandringham from Windsor Great Park when it was found he would be suitable for training. Together with Donna, who was bought as a puppy, he alternates with one of the Queen's spaniels on shooting days. The spaniels are perfect for working close to their handler while the larger Labradors cover the areas further afield.

There is a natural hunting instinct in breeds such as gun dogs, hounds and even terriers. The royal family has traditionally owned gun dogs, a category that includes retrievers, pointers, setters, spaniels and even, surprising to some, poodles, all of which are bred to work on a one-to-one basis, which is why they become so loyal to their handlers. Among the current pack of spaniels at Sandringham are five great favourites: Lily, Duster, Shrimp, Muskett and Monty.

And even though many of those breeds are still regarded very much as working dogs who have to earn their keep, there are still some who are now kept as personal pets, particularly spaniels and poodles. You only have to look at the men and women who walk their dogs every day to see the wide variety of animals that were once only kept as working dogs but are now regarded as part of the family and live comfortably within the household.

The only small breeds the Duke of Edinburgh tolerates are terriers who have been developed in Britain only since the early twentieth century, first because they were excellent and cheap rat catchers at a time when the country was overrun with the vermin, and more recently as good hunters of foxes when the sport was permissible.

The terriers' diminutive size and total fearlessness made them into superb 'foragers' as they followed a quarry into places the bigger dogs could not fit. They would then drive the fox – or any other target – out into the open for the hounds to chase before the hunt caught up. Terriers also possess an acute sense of hearing which enabled them to track down a quarry long before any horse or human ear could hear a sound.

After spending most of the winter months at Sandringham, later in the year the working dogs are transported to Balmoral in time for the start of the grouse season when, once again, as the Queen and her family are in residence, large house parties are invited to shoot.

In between, the dogs are involved in gun dog trials throughout the country, with their handlers being the kennel staff at Sandringham. If the events are being held fairly near Sandringham, the Queen and the Duke of Edinburgh will often turn up to watch their teams perform.

When any of the Labradors produce a litter of puppies, the Queen decides how many, if any, are to be sold, and she also insists on giving her approval to whomever wishes to buy the puppies. Money is important – the animals can fetch thousands of pounds each, particularly when buyers realise they have an opportunity to own one of Her Majesty's dogs – and the undoubted quality of their breeding, and the kennels have to pay their way.

The Queen's working dogs like to be busy and they have a routine organised by the kennel master at Sandringham, months in advance. He knows when they will be required on the estate, particularly for one of the biggest days of the year, the Duke of Edinburgh's shooting party which he has always held on Boxing Day since the Queen came to the throne. This is the day when all male guests who shoot (and others are rarely invited) spend all day in the fields while the beaters raise the birds that are fetched by the dogs, all the time watched by the ladies in the party. It is a splendid day's sport for those who enjoy the activity and the 'picnic' atmosphere as they all join together for al fresco dining and drinks if it is a dry day. The only thing that can spoil the occasion is if it rains, as it usually does in Norfolk. Not that the royal family care about the weather, but it does make eating and drinking al fresco slightly uncomfortable; even more so for the servants who have to serve.

Prince Edward, the Earl of Wessex, is an excellent shot and when he is at Sandringham he likes to take Bracken, one of the Queen's yellow Labradors, out with him. The dog is a natural hunter and it is a mark of royal pride that several of his puppies have been taken to Australia, where they are used by the police and customs officers as 'sniffer' dogs, with brilliant results.

As the Queen and the Duke of Edinburgh continue to breed gun dogs at Sandringham, their attachment to dogs is apparent to everyone who knows them. Indeed, it is said by others to be an inspiration to anyone who is considering owning a dog – of whatever breed!

15

Royal Show Dogs

Royal owners from Queen Victoria to the present day have competed successfully at Crufts, the world's premier dog show, with every sovereign owning a winning animal.

The value attached to a winning dog multiplies when it comes with a royal connection and the interest in breeding continues to be undiminished.

Members of the royal family have been active supporters of various dog shows since Edward, the Prince of Wales, and the then Princess Alexandra entered a number of their dogs in the International Dog Show in London in 1863, when there were fifty-seven classes and over 600 entries. The support has never wavered.

Among the animals Edward and Alexandra exhibited

were two borzois, a Newfoundland, an Indian mastiff and a Russian retriever. There were no pure-bred British dogs at that time.

Edward became patron of the Kennel Club in 1873 and he was pleased when Charles Cruft organised his first show at the Royal Aquarium in London in 1889.

Two years later, Cruft moved his show to the Royal Agricultural Hall in Islington, in 1891. With 500 entries and thirty-five different breeds on show, the competition began its period as the most important dog show in the world, an unchallenged position it still holds today.

Cruft, an astute businessman as well as a dog lover – his day-time job was as sales manager for Spratts, the dog biscuit manufacturers – realised that with royal participation he was guaranteed success. With an eye to the future, and further regal patronage, he chose as the design for the medallions of the winners a likeness of Queen Victoria's collie, Darnley II, surmounted by the British crown.

Her Majesty had entered her collie in addition to three Pomeranians, Gena, Fluffy and Nino, all of which, surprisingly, won prizes. At the same show Edward entered four basset hounds which were also successful.

In one sweep, Cruft, a consummate showman, had assured himself of continued success and international recognition. He continued to run the show until his death in 1938, when his widow took over the organisation. But four years later she found it was too much for her alone, and she sold Crufts to the Kennel Club, who have owned and run it ever since.

One of the extra commercial benefits of royal interest in dog shows was an increased awareness of the public in the breeds they favoured, which became highly sought after both in Britain and abroad.

In the first years of the twentieth century, a collie that had won first prize at Crufts could easily fetch over £1,000. And this was at a time when the average weekly wage in Britain was less than £2.

Then, as now, royalty attracted attention wherever it went and whatever it did. Members of the royal family didn't have to do anything; they simply had to be there. The rarest, and certainly most expensive, dogs in Britain were borzois and when Queen Alexandra exhibited her favourite, Alix, people would queue for hours just to obtain a glimpse of this magnificent animal.

During the period of Victoria's vast Empire, foreign monarchs and princes vied with each other to obtain dogs favoured by the British royal family. Money was no object and in India, in particular, maharajas spared no expense on prize pedigree dogs. They all sent representatives to Crufts with open chequebooks and instructions to buy as many of the prize winners as possible.

One Indian potentate, the Maharaja of Patiala, had more than 100 British-bred dogs at one time, including Labradors, spaniels and fox terriers.

The First World War instilled in the British people an instant hatred of all things German, including animals. The dachshund, which had long been Queen Victoria's favourite breed, disappeared almost overnight. George V said it was a blessing his grandmother had not lived to see the day. The German shepherd dog was renamed the Alsatian, to give it a French identity, Alsace being French in origin before being annexed by Germany. Ironically, the breed later became the favourite of Adolf Hitler.

It wasn't until the war had ended that the Kennel Club officially recognised the German shepherd dog – and then only as the 'Alsatian'. In 1920, the then Prince of Wales (later Edward VIII) bestowed the official royal seal of approval on the breed when he entered his Alsatian, Claus of Seale, at Crufts.

George V supported Crufts and in 1916 he entered his three-year-old Labrador bitch, Wolferton Jet, winning first prize. The dog went on to win a number of awards that year, including the Kennel Club Challenge Certificate at Manchester.

His Majesty then did the double at the Sandy Championship Show with Wolferton Ben and Wolferton Sheila.

George V's successor, Edward VIII, supported Crufts for many years. His first entry at the show was Gwen, his Welsh terrier, who won first prize.

As Duke of Windsor, following the abdication, he

did not again enter at Crufts or any other dog show in Britain, but both he and the duchess showed their favourite pugs, Goldengleam Trooper and Pugvilles Imperial (who was known by his pet name Imp), first of all in Europe and later in the United States where they invariably won prizes.

All of George V's sons exhibited at Crufts including the Duke of Kent (father of the present duke), whose pride and joy was his Great Dane Ch. Midas of Send.

In 1934, Prince Henry, Duke of Gloucester, and his wife Princess Alice paid a visit to Australia and on their return they brought with them two Australian terriers. It was the start of a love affair with the breed that would last for over fifty years.

The duke was appointed governor general of Australia in 1945 at the conclusion of the Second World War and when the couple returned to England in 1947 they brought more Australian terriers: Kursal Blue Piper and Kursal Blue Jean. Princess Alice took over the breeding programme to make sure the terriers retained their 'Australianness'. Her Royal Highness became very knowledgeable about the breed and the last one she owned died in 1978 and was buried in the animal cemetery at Barnwell Manor, the Gloucesters' country home in Northamptonshire.

King George VI decided to enter one of his black Labradors, Sandringham Stream, at the King's Lynn Show in 1939, winning a cup for best gun dog.

His Majesty was extremely proud of the achievements of his gun dogs at trials and, in particular, of Windsor Bob at the Kennel Club's open Retriever Trial at Sutton Scotney in Hampshire in 1948. He had been bred, trained and handled by the head keeper at Windsor.

In 1956, the Duke of Edinburgh bred Sandringham Mint, who won two novice stakes. Among the kennel's other successes were the Queen's Sandringham Ranger, Sandringham Slipper, Sandringham Sydney and Sandringham Salt, all of whom won awards and prizes.

Then in 1997, the Princess Royal, reviving interest in the Clumber spaniels, entered her bitch, Tinglestone Spot Scherzando, in the special field trial event for the breed. It didn't win first prize but the fact that a member of the royal family had entered a Clumber in the first place conferred that extra mantle of success on the breed.

Kennel Club records reveal that since coming to the throne, Her Majesty has registered her gun dogs practically every year and entered many of them in shows and trials throughout the country.

In Coronation Year, 1953, the Queen registered two of her retriever Labradors with amusing names she had chosen herself: Sandringham Topsy and Sandringham Turvey.

Among other Labradors she registered with the Kennel Club have been: Sandringham Hugo, Sandringham Tatler, Sandringham Hill, Sandringham Salt, Sandringham Collar, Sandringham Rock, Sandringham Vesper and Topper of Sandringham.

But royal interest in exhibiting at Crufts declined after the Second World War – the show having been suspended during the period of hostilities. However, Elizabeth II visited Crufts Dog Show on Friday

7 February 1969, the first time a reigning monarch had visited the show. (In 1947, when she was still, of course, Princess Elizabeth, Her Royal Highness visited the Welsh Corgi League Show.)

And among her winners at various other trials were Sandringham Boost, who took several first places, and Sandringham Spark, another success story.

Contrary to what many people believe, dog shows are not beauty contests. Witness some of the best-in-show winners in recent years when the top prize has been awarded to an animal only its mother would consider handsome.

Obedience and behaviour are of paramount importance but, in fairness, it must be admitted that all those in the final line-up love showing off and they all have supreme self-confidence in their own ability. In other words, they know they look good and they want the spectators to appreciate them, even if the owners of their competitors sometimes have to fight hard to maintain their smiles when they are beaten into second and third places.

There has always been fierce competition among dog owners to see who can claim to have the biggest, smallest, smoothest and most obedient – in other words, the best. This is why, in 1873, the British Kennel Club was founded by a group of enthusiasts in order that acknowledged experts in the various breeds could establish specific criteria by which individual animals could be judged.

The Kennel Club – they don't have to call it the 'British KC' as everyone knows there is only one supreme organisation – was, and remains, the standard for all breeds of dog, with the American Kennel Club being formed in 1884 and the Canadian club four years later.

The Queen's own preference is for field trials where her gun dogs are put through their paces under the watchful eyes of experienced judges who are not in the least bit intimidated by the owner's status or rank.

She also enjoys sheepdog trials where a flock is herded by a single dog over a pre-set course and must herd the sheep into an enclosure without any barking or 'nipping' at ankles. Every sheepdog handler knows that patience is required as points are awarded for speed, but they are also deducted if the handler has to do too much of the exercise. To watch an expert at work is to witness a master class in teamwork between man and beast, carried out with the minimum of fuss and total silence, apart from the whistle. This is one event where silence really is golden.

Perhaps one of the most appealing aspects of field trials, certainly from the Queen's point of view, is that there is never a large financial prize. The real enthusiast is a true amateur, there simply for the honour of the award, the excitement and also the pleasure of meeting other handlers who share their interests and passions.

In Britain, animal breeding had been the sole prerogative of the nobility for centuries. Confined mainly to horses, both for racing and hunting, and large dogs, which were also used for hunting, the custom was introduced for practical reasons rather than for the rearing of pets.

If King Edward VII could see what Crufts has become in the twenty-first century he would be delighted that the institution he supported in its infancy has developed into the major international dog show in the world – and it is still supported by royalty!

16

Bereavement

The death of a pet has reduced even the most hard-ened royal to a state of deep emotion and grief. For over 500 years bereaved royal pet owners have mourned the loss of their animals, be they working horses, hunters or just tiny lapdogs with no practical use or value. Kings, queens, princes and princesses have lavished praise on their pets they would not dream of attributing to any human being, even members of their own family.

Queen Victoria would not allow any of her pets to be destroyed, no matter how diseased they were or if the vets attending them advised it was the best course.

In 1881 when her favourite collie of the moment, Noble, fell ill, she didn't trust her vet, Charles Rotherham, so she summoned her own doctor, Sir James Reid, to make a diagnosis. Both prescribed medication and the dog survived for another three years, eventually dying at the grand old age of sixteen in 1884.

Sir James wrote that:

> Her Majesty was much upset, and cried a great deal, said she was so fond of those that were gone, and that everything in the world comes to an end ... she could not bear to go and see his body, though she would have liked to kiss his head ... I had to increase the strength of her sleeping draught...

Queen Victoria wrote in her diaries of the deep sadness she felt whenever one of her pets died. When her childhood favourite spaniel, Dash, died on Christmas Eve 1840, just three years after Victoria ascended the throne, the Queen had her buried in the garden of Adelaide Cottage in Windsor Home Park – now the home of one of the Queen's most senior household. Part of her personal message to all who might read the inscription on the headstone she erected to her beloved favourite little dog says it all about her true feelings.

READER

IF YOU WOULD BE BELOVED AND DIE REGRETTED

PROFIT BY THE EXAMPLE OF

DASH

Four years later when Eos, Prince Albert's ten-year-old greyhound, died, he was buried in a small brick grave, lead lined, which was then placed under a statue of Queen Victoria at Windsor.

Victoria believed dogs had souls and that they all went to Heaven when they died. Even so, she grieved a great deal when one of them passed on and often said how short their lives were. In fact, when Däckel, her favourite dachshund, died in 1860 at the age of fifteen, she mourned the loss, exclaiming, 'These charming creatures live so short a time.' Another favourite, Dandie Dinmont, was actually nineteen when she died in 1858, an amazing age for any dog.

The death of a royal owner was also often mourned by its pet. When Queen Victoria was plainly failing in 1901, her favourite Pomeranian, Turi, came and sat beside her on her bed. When she finally died the animal whined and had to be physically removed.

The royal pets have been buried in their own cemeteries since Queen Victoria created a graveyard in a quiet corner of the 20,000-acre Sandringham estate, initially for her beloved collie Noble. The Duke of Windsor recalled how many memorials there were to Queen Victoria's animals at Balmoral: '…every turn of the paths brought one face to face with a statue, inscribed granite, drinking fountain or seat dedicated to the memory of a relation or a faithful retainer or even a pet dog'.

There is little doubt that the utter desolation felt by many dog owners when their pet dies equals if not surpasses that which they feel when a human friend goes. This is perhaps why so many animal epitaphs are so heart-rending and touching.

The duke died of cancer in 1972 with his pug, Black Diamond, lying beside him on his bed. The dog did not last long after his master, dying of the same disease.

Royal and aristocratic children often gave their pets identities other children would give to their toys. When the Queen Mother was a young girl, the daughter of the Earl of Strathmore, she had a pet bullfinch that she regarded as hers and hers alone with no other member of her family permitted to chat to it the way she did. And when the bird died, having been eaten by one of the family's cats, the young Elizabeth decided, along with her brother David, to stage a proper funeral. They found a pencil box in the nursery that became the coffin and after carefully placing the bullfinch inside, she and her brother bore the coffin, with due solemnity, in a procession into the woods at their home, where David dug a grave and then stood in respectful silence as Elizabeth intoned a funeral service she had made up. A cross was placed over the grave after they had sung a children's song, as they didn't know the words to any hymn without the book.

As previously mentioned, Princess Elizabeth and her sister Margaret owned a chameleon for a time. It was an unusual pet for the royal children but they had hours of enjoyment with it and when it finally became ill and had to be sent to live with one of the gatekeepers who knew how to care for it, they were desolate. And even more so when they heard it had died.

Princess Elizabeth, taking charge, decided that a proper burial was required, so a large white box was found and the chameleon was buried in the garden under a flowering shrub, while the two princesses sang a hymn and said a prayer. In organising the burial, the children were following the example of their mother, who when she was their age and with her brother carried out similar ceremonials for their pets.

Margaret also kept a tortoise and liked to watch in the garden as the dogs attempted to eat it. She laughed when they all failed to get through the shell. When the tortoise died, Margaret insisted it should be given a proper burial and a quiet spot was found where the animal could be laid to rest. She organised the ceremony and marked the spot with a tiny cross, only to find shortly afterwards that one of the family's dogs had managed to dig up the grave and was seen trotting across the lawn with the corpse in its mouth. She dragged the remains out of the dog's mouth and found another, more secluded spot for a second burial. This time none of the dogs found it.

More than seventy years after Queen Victoria started the first pet cemetery, her great-great-granddaughter, Elizabeth II was looking for a suitable spot to bury her first corgi, Susan, who had died in January 1959, also at Sandringham. She remembered from her child-hood the pets' graveyard, which is separated from the rest of the estate by a stone wall in which plaques commemorating the names of deceased dogs are inset. It has since become the largest of the pets' cemeteries.

Whenever one of the Queen's favourite animals dies, she takes a few minutes alone to remember them, and even longer to compose suitable words that will be inscribed on their tombstones.

The Queen's corgis are usually buried in whichever royal residence they happen to be in when they die. The exception is Buckingham Palace where there is no animal cemetery as the public are admitted to the grounds during the summer openings. The Queen prefers her pets to lie at rest in a peaceful corner, where she can visit them quietly. As well as Susan, both Sugar and Heather are also buried at Sandringham, where they died, with inscribed headstones to mark their graves.

During the course of her life, the Queen has owned more than thirty corgis, all of them descended from Susan. And when that first pet died on 26 January 1959, Her Majesty made several sketches for a proposed memorial gravestone. It wasn't enough just to record the name and date of death. Robert Marrington, at that time the person responsible for such matters in the crown estate, had inscribed the headstone, 'Susan, died

26th January 1959, for 15 years the faithful companion of the Queen.'

On reading this, Her Majesty discovered a slight inaccuracy in that Susan had in fact been born on 18 February 1944, so she had not quite completed the full fifteen years' service.

The Queen then instructed Mr Marrington to change the inscription to include the date of birth and added the word 'almost' before '15 years'. Such is Her Majesty's legendary attention to detail.

There was later a suggestion that the Queen's sketches should be sold at auction in 2004. But before the sale could take place, officials from the royal household took action and prevented the sketches being offered. They now rest in the Royal Archives. If they had been sold publicly, they would have realised very large sums.

Two of Susan's descendants, Sugar and Heather, have headstones bearing similar epitaphs, 'The faithful companion of the Queen', with the words added that 'they were great-granddaughters of Susan'.

The Queen has a whole line of tombstones at Sandringham where her working dogs are all buried, in addition to the corgis, with each one bearing the prefix Sandringham. Each of the inscriptions on the headstones has either been written by the Queen or approved by her or another royal pet owner and, as well as recording the dates of the dog's life, each one gives an insight into the character of the animal buried there. Hence:

H.M. THE QUEEN'S

SANDRINGHAM SYDNEY

14.5.70–2.5.82

SYDNEY WAS AN HONEST WORKER,

A FAITHFUL COMPANION

AND WILL BE MISSED BY ALL.

N.B. Sandringham Sydney had been Field Trial Champion in 1979.

SANDRINGHAM SALT

DEVOTED AND ALWAYS WILLING TO WORK

SANDRINGHAM BRAE

A GENTLEMAN AMONGST DOGS

SANDRINGHAM FERN

TIRELESS WORKER AND MISCHIEVOUS CHARACTER

One of the earliest graves during the Queen's reign was that of Prince Philip's yellow Labrador Candy, who His Royal Highness had owned since 1952, Accession

Year, and who had been a loyal companion until he died in 1958.

Of all the British monarchs, few could match the devotion of Edward VII to his dogs.

He was heartbroken when his pet French toy bulldog, Peter, had to be destroyed after being run over by a butcher's cart on the eve of the coronation in 1902. His vet, A. J. Sewell, found a replacement, the rough-haired terrier Jack, and when he too came to an untimely end, having choked to death while eating, the King ordered that some of Jack's hair should be made into a bracelet which from then on occupied a place of honour on His Majesty's desk.

Edward VII was unlucky with several of his pet dogs. Jack's successor was an Irish terrier who was diagnosed with cancer and had to be put down to save him from excruciating pain.

Edward had been given his first dog, a retriever called Duck, when he was eleven. He adored the animal and when he died in 1854, the prince recorded in his diary: 'Unfortunately today poor Duck died having been with me 1 year and a ¼, he was six years old, and I am sure I never saw or knew a nicer dog.'

When Edward married Princess Alexandra, he was delighted to find that she shared his love of animals. Her own favourite dog at the time was a Pekingese, Togo, and when it died in 1914 she was inconsolable, refusing to leave her room or eat anything. She insisted on having the dog laid on a cushion in her bedroom where for several days she looked at it and sobbed uncontrollably. Eventually, the smell of the decomposing body became so overpowering that a lady-in-waiting persuaded Her Majesty to allow a page to remove it as it was a health hazard, with typhoid a real danger. The following day a new Peke was produced to replace Togo and the Queen rapidly recovered.

Togo was buried at Marlborough House, in Pall Mall, now the Commonwealth Headquarters in London, and Alexandra had the following words engraved on his tombstone:

MY DARLING LITTLE TOGO. GIVEN TO ME BY THE
EMPRESS OF JAPAN. MY CONSTANT COMPANION
FOR 12 YEARS. THE JOY AND PLEASURE OF MY LIFE.
DIED MAY 25TH 1914.

When the famous Caesar came on the scene in 1907 he quickly became inseparable from the King. So when the dog became ill during a royal visit to Marienbad, Edward wanted his own personal vet, Sewell, brought out from London. It was pointed out to him that the cost would be over £200, equivalent to £20,000 today. The King didn't care about the cost; all he wanted was the very best treatment available. Eventually he was persuaded to allow a local man to treat Caesar, with excellent results.

Four years after Edward's death in 1910, during which time Caesar had remained a firm favourite with his widow, he died in April 1914, following an operation. During his final hours, Alexandra was at his side constantly, soothing him and stroking his head. She then arranged for Caesar to be buried in the animal cemetery she had established in the garden at Marlborough House, which had been her London home since Edward's death in 1910.

Queen Alexandra placed flowers on the dog's grave regularly and she also wrote the words that were inscribed on his tombstone:

OUR BELOVED CAESAR WHO WAS THE KING'S
FAITHFUL AND CONSTANT COMPANION UNTIL
DEATH AND MY GREATEST COMFORTER IN MY
LONELINESS AND SORROW FOR FOUR YEARS AFTER.
DIED APRIL 18TH 1914.

In 1918, Alexandra arranged, with the permission of her son, King George V, for Caesar to be reunited with his royal master, at least figuratively, when a carving of the dog was added to the king's tomb in St George's Chapel at Windsor Castle.

Many animal lovers claim to have a sixth sense between them and their pets. The Queen's uncle, the Duke of Kent, who was killed in a wartime aircraft crash in August 1942, seemed to have a strange premonition of his own death. When he left his country house Coppins, he stroked his chow-chow, Muff, and said to his butler, Bysouth, 'What will you do with him when I am gone?'

British sovereigns have showed their sadness at the loss of a beloved pet in many ways, but none has gone quite as far as some foreign monarchs and their consorts.

When Marie Henriette, the wife of King Leopold II of Belgium, died in 1902, she left a legacy of £2,000 – an enormous sum in those days – to her pet griffon and to a servant, with instructions to care for the animal for the rest of its life.

Such is the affection that royalty has felt and still feels for their pets that no one found anything out of the ordinary in this bequest.

17

Feathered Friends

Most people in Britain – those from the south anyway – imagine that anyone who has anything to do with racing pigeons must be from the north of England, wear a cloth cap and a muffler around his neck and spend all his waking hours petting his birds in a makeshift loft at the bottom of his garden – if he is lucky enough to have a garden. In other words, it has traditionally been a lower-working-class pastime only practised by those who cannot afford anything better.

The idea that not only the aristocracy but royalty are passionate about pigeon racing, and have been for generations, would not only surprise the vast majority of the population, but might not be believed.

The truth is that the Queen is not only the owner and breeder of one of the most successful pigeon-racing lofts in the United Kingdom, she knows as much about the habits and welfare of her birds as the most dedicated pigeon fancier anywhere in the country.

And it didn't all start with the Queen. Her great-grandfather, King Edward VII, was the first member of the royal family to enter the sport back in the nineteenth century when he was still Prince of Wales, and each successive monarch has continued his interest.

Paying visitors to Sandringham during the season sometimes ask where the royal pigeon lofts are. Well, they are not actually inside the Sandringham estate, but just outside the boundary wall in the village of West Newton, where they are under the supervision of a gentleman who has been given the rather grand title of royal lofts manager.

At the time of writing, around 160 mature pigeons are housed in the royal lofts at Sandringham, along with a further eighty young birds. While the majority are kept for racing, others in the lofts are there as breeding stock.

They are entered into several races every week – it doesn't do to allow the birds to get lazy – and the Queen's birds compete in all national races during the season, which runs from April to September.

Records show that the Queen is among the most successful owners and breeders, with her pigeons having won
every major race in the United Kingdom over the years.

Her Majesty has graciously agreed to become president or patron of a number of pigeon-racing societies
in recognition of her interest in the sport, including the
National Flying Association.

The Royal Pigeon Racing Association, of which she
is patron, has its headquarters in Cheltenham, where a
pigeon has pride of place on the town's coat-of-arms.
The RPRA is the premier organisation for pigeon
racing in the United Kingdom, with many affiliations
overseas. Indeed, it was because pigeons were seen
pecking at the soil back in the eighteenth century that
the famous spa water wells were discovered, becoming popular with one of the Queen's ancestors, King
George III. The royal connection with pigeons is well
over 200 years old.

Today, the RPRA is a thriving business with over
thirty full-time employees and an annual turnover in
excess of £1.2 million.

On 28 March 1896, there was a meeting of 'pigeon keep-ers' at the White Swan public house in Leeds for the purpose of forming a homing league, which in turn led to the formation of the National Homing Union. The title 'Royal' was not added until much later, but there was a close affinity with members of the royal family from the earliest days. Indeed, it was not until the end of the Second World War that the organisation became the Royal National Homing Union, later to become what it is today, the Royal Pigeon Racing Association (RPRA).

In 1886, King Leopold II of the Belgians entertained Edward, Prince of Wales, during a visit to Belgium, which is recognised as the true home of racing pigeons.

Edward admired Leopold's birds and, when he returned to England, he found that Leopold had selected some of his prize pigeons – of the Delmotte-Jurion strain – and dispatched them as a gift to Sandringham, which has been the home of the sovereign's flight ever since.

However, Edward quickly lost his enthusiasm for his latest acquisition and seven years passed before royal interest was revived by his son the Duke of York (long before he became King George V), who decided to become involved in the sport.

In 1893, George decided to build a proper racing loft to accommodate some of the Belgian birds and their offspring in the grounds of his home, York Cottage, which was a short walk from Sandringham House. George and his wife loved York Cottage so much that even after he succeeded to the throne, it wasn't until 1935 that he was persuaded to leave the house and move into the main property at Sandringham House. York Cottage today is the Sandringham Estate Office.

On hearing that his son was becoming successful with his pigeons, Edward, who could never resist a challenge, ordered another, better and bigger racing loft to be built for himself so that training of his birds could begin in earnest. He was determined that his pigeons would be faster and more successful than anyone else's, including his son's.

There was serious rivalry between the two royal lofts and not always of the friendly variety usually associated with the sport.

Both Edward and his son hated to lose and in 1899, in an important race from Lerwick in the Shetland Isles (a distance of over 500 miles), Edward triumphed with his entry coming in first ahead of the duke's third- and fifth-placed birds.

The difference in attitude between the two royal fanciers was that whereas Edward was content to leave the training and breeding of his birds to his handlers, but making sure he always turned up to accept the prizes when any of them won, the Duke of York was a true pigeon fancier and took a personal interest in every aspect of the sport. He knew the name, number and pedigree of every bird and loved few things more than spending hours in the company of other enthusiasts. In the truest sense, he really was a 'hands-on' pigeon fancier – and his love of his birds lasted throughout his life. Even when he ascended the throne in 1910, he continued to be fascinated by his homing birds and, monarchical duties permitting, he loved nothing more than to hear how they were progressing. And this carried on throughout the darkest days of the First World War, when he was proud to volunteer his birds to act as carrier pigeons in France.

During the Second World War, homing pigeons were seconded once more into the National Pigeon Service and the royal pigeons were volunteered by King George VI. One of his birds was awarded the Dickin Medal for Gallantry, the equivalent of the Victoria Cross for pigeons, for its role in reporting a lost aircraft. On 10 October 1940, his pigeon Royal Blue was released in Holland from an aircraft that had been force-landed and flew 120 miles in four hours and ten minutes, to report the situation of the aircraft and its crew. It was the first time a pigeon had brought home a message from a stranded crew in occupied Europe. In 1943, the Dickin Medal was instituted by Maria Dickin, founder of the People's Dispensary for Sick Animals (PDSA), and her medal was awarded to fifty-three animals, of which thirty-two were homing pigeons. Royal Blue was the first to be honoured, in March 1945.

The pigeons would travel in the skies across occupied Europe and into Germany on board RAF bombers and at the conclusion of a raid they would be released to fly home with vital information secreted in the rings attached to their legs. Occasionally, some were even dropped by parachute to waiting Resistance workers on the ground, who would then attach the necessary information and release the bird.

Back in the days when George V was still a young Duke of York, he was responsible for the appointment of the first official royal pigeon handler when he persuaded his father to allow both of their lofts to merge under the care of a Mr Jones, who, as well as being a veteran pigeon fancier, had also been village schoolmaster at nearby West Newton since 1881.

The birds were divided into two categories: racing and breeding. For racing it was important that the stock included established long-distance winners, and for breeding, older birds were needed who could 'foster' the young pigeons until they were ready to leave the nest.

The royal lofts are among the most comfortable built anywhere. They are not luxurious, but large enough for the handlers to stand upright and still be able to reach any of the birds. They are light and airy with plenty of room for each bird to fly and perch and, as one would expect, they are ultra-clean.

The reasons for their comfortable quarters is twofold: one, they have to be hygienic for health reasons, and two, the racing pigeons have to want to return home as quickly as possible in order to make them top racing birds.

There was a four-year period in the early stages of the Queen's reign when she did not take an active interest in her lofts due to the pressures of learning the business of monarchy. No royal birds raced during that time. Later Her Majesty found time to involve herself and since then she has become extremely knowledgeable about her racing pigeons and even names some of them herself, as she does with most of her other animal interests.

Today, some of her better birds are worth well over £1,000 and not because of their royal provenance. In the world of racing pigeons, rank counts for little; it's the quality of the birds that matters, and those at Sandringham are as good as any in the world.

Epilogue

So what if the Queen prefers the company of her pets to most humans? It is entirely her choice. She is a woman who, for most of her adult life, has been in the ultimate male world, one that is dominated by men who believe they know better than her, even if they are wary about showing their true feelings.

So it is perfectly understandable if she likes to leave the cares and worries of constitutional monarchy behind her from time to time, and retreat to the comfort of her corgis, spaniels, Labradors and horses.

The Queen occupies a unique position in that only with her husband can she be truly unguarded. Even with her own children and grandchildren, there is always a certain amount of reservation. So, with her animals she is able to relax completely in the knowledge that they cannot repeat anything they see or hear. Their companionship is almost impossible to understand by outsiders, but to her they are able to help relieve the tensions and frustrations that inevitably occur from time to time when one is a constitutional monarch who dares not voice personal opinions.

Her Majesty's deep attachment to her animals means she knows each one by name and that includes all the corgis she has owned since 1944 and her pack of gun dogs at Sandringham. The Queen is also able to recall the names of every pony and horse she has ridden since childhood, through to the hacks she still rides at weekends at Windsor; all her racehorses; and even the thirty or so Windsor Greys (the carriage horses) in the royal mews. It is a remarkable achievement.

For centuries dogs have been kept by royalty for several purposes: hunting, guarding people and property, working with livestock and acting as dependable, loyal companions.

The changes we have witnessed in the kinds of dogs the royal family has owned over the years are due largely to selective breeding. In the Queen's case, her corgis have had the 'snappiness' bred out of them in the thirty or so animals she has owned. At least, that is the theory, but try telling that to some of the footmen and housemaids at Buckingham Palace, many of whom have been bitten by the 'gentle' creatures.

The Queen's attention to detail is legendary. It extends from the decorations worn by members of the household, in the correct order and what each represents, to the equipment used by mounted officers of the household brigade when they are parading before a formal ceremony. She is very aware of the strain hours on parade can mean to a horse as well as the soldiers and her concern for the animals often is more vocal than that used for the officers and guardsmen. As she says, the humans are able to voice their complaints, the horses cannot.

She was once heard to remark to her Silver-Stick-in-Waiting – her closest escort whenever she is either riding or being driven in a horse-drawn carriage – that an 'officer is riding a bit short'. She was referring to the fact that the officer concerned had his stirrups a little too far forward and was not mounted in the correct position, which could have placed an unnecessary strain on the horse, or certainly made the ride more uncomfortable for both.

Nothing escapes her attention and it is little details like these that make those around her sit up straighter and make sure all is in order before going on parade.

Her Majesty does not make these comments just to air her superiority, neither has she acquired all her knowledge of horses and horsemanship from equestrian books, though she has read many of the leading publications on the subject. Everything she knows about horses she has learned from personal experience and every crown equerry who has served her also knows that she knows what she is talking about because, in nearly every instance, she has done it before. After all, she has been there longer than any of them!

And, in exactly the same way that she learned to handle a horse with increasing confidence as she was growing up, she has made sure that her own children and grandchildren learn to enjoy the fun and happiness that comes with riding their ponies and horses. What is more, she has instilled in them the joy of experiencing the total freedom that comes from a pastime, perhaps the only one, where they are free from the intrusion of a voracious media and public.

Like every other dog owner in this nation of dog lovers, the Queen believes in her heart that hers and hers alone are the best in the world. She also believes, like most dog owners, that her pets are endowed with many human and even super-human qualities. According to her they have a conscience, with a sense of guilt when they have done something wrong, and they can understand her moods when she is feeling sad, happy, angry or despondent.

Her Majesty says her corgis and Labradors are able to communicate with her through their behaviour and even by the tone of their barking. She believes, again like every other dog owner, that dogs are not mere animals, but something much more. She knows when they feel lonely and they understand when she is preparing to leave them. They sense when something out of the ordinary is about to happen – and they hate to be left alone in the house – or Palace!

The Queen's continued interest in animals, be they domestic pets or those, such as her racing pigeons and working dogs, which are kept mainly for their sporting prowess, is an indication of the manner in which royalty has kept alive their love of all creatures, four legged and feathered, through the generations.

Her devotion to her corgis, Labradors, spaniels and horses shows a genuine and touching attachment to her pets that has stood the test of time – and shows no sign of diminishing.

So, perhaps, as we say 'Long live the Queen', we might also add 'and her pets'. They are the companions who continue to show unbounded love and loyalty and, in her case, they are truly a Queen's best friend.

Appendix 1
Royal Animal Patronages

It was as Duke of York, that Bertie, later King George VI, addressed the International Humane Congress in London in 1924 to mark the centenary of the RSPCA. Among his remarks, he said, 'I believe the reason that today so many people are genuine animal lovers can largely be traced to the beneficent educational activity of the RSPCA.'

Both Queen Victoria and King Edward VII supported many animal charities and passed on their patronages to their heirs in due course. Where royalty goes, the mass of the population follows. It has always been the case and there is no sign of it diminishing. There is nothing like having a member of the royal family involved in a charity or society for it to become fashionable and for the public purse to be opened up as a result.

Nearly every member of the present royal family is associated with some sort of animal charity or organisation. Officials of these bodies all realise that to have a royal name on their letter heads guarantees public interest – and increased revenue!

The Queen is patron of over thirty, ranging from the RSPCA to the Labrador Retriever Club, with the Red Poll Cattle Society and the Royal Pigeon Racing Association among the diverse interests she enjoys.

She became patron of the Animal Health Trust in 1959. The trust was founded in 1942 and received its Royal Charter in 1963. Its aim is to diagnose and treat all forms of animal disease in horses, cats and dogs.

The largest dog welfare charity by far is the Dogs Trust, which was founded in 1891. Each year it cares for up to 16,000 dogs. Her Majesty is an active patron, not merely a figurehead.

The oldest of the animal charities is Battersea Dogs Home, which was founded in 1860. In 1883 it began to care for cats, too, and royal patronage followed in 1884. In 2002 it was renamed Battersea Dogs and Cats Home.

The Queen has been patron of Battersea Dogs Home since 1956 and Prince Michael of Kent has been the president since 1984. Battersea is one of the most recognised of all animal charities and it cares for 20,000 dogs every year and up to 900 cats.

Perhaps the RSPCA, the Royal Society for the Prevention of Cruelty to Animals, is better known by its initials. Catering for the welfare of all animals, including reptiles, birds and insects, the society receives on average some 1.5 million telephone calls every year and, as patron, the Queen receives an annual report from its officers which last year revealed that the cat population of the United Kingdom was approximately eight million, with the dog population surprisingly exactly the same number.

As a successful owner and breeder of racehorses, it is not too surprising to find Her Majesty is patron of the Thoroughbred Breeders' Association, and, considering the royal family's long-time love affair with all things equestrian, her patronage of the Royal Windsor Horse Show is a given. This is one of the best-attended horse shows in Britain and several equestrian charities benefit by having stalls around the ground. If the Queen, the Duke of Edinburgh, the Prince of Wales or the Princess Royal happen to call in during one of their obligatory walks around the exhibits, they are surrounded by spectators who then automatically reach for their wallets to buy a souvenir or simply to offer money for the good cause.

Now, of course, it is the Duke and Duchess of Cambridge and Prince Harry who are the focus of much public attention at these events, and a much younger crowd is attracted just because of their presence. They do not object to the men, women and children who follow them around at an event that is being held for charity; it's the media with their intrusive camera lenses they dislike.

The Queen is also patron of the Peterborough Royal Foxhound Show Society; the British Horse Society; the Highland Pony Society, in which she takes a particular interest because of her passion for the breeding and purity of Highland ponies; the Kennel Club; and the Labrador Retriever Club (as a successful owner and breeder of Labrador retrievers at Sandringham, this is another natural organisation for Her Majesty).

The Duke of Edinburgh has a string of patronages, presidencies and memberships relating to animals, birds and sea life including the British Falconers' Club, the Cornell University Laboratory of Ornithology and Birds Australia, Friends of the Sea Otter, 1001: A Nature Trust, the Asian Institute of Technology Club, the Fell Pony Society (which as its name implies cares for the welfare of all fell ponies that roam the northern fells), the Quebec Wildlife Foundation, Friends of the Serengeti (looking after the fate of East Africa's wildlife), the Game and Wildlife Conservation Trust, the French Society for the Protection of Horses, the Royal International Whale Safari Club, the Royal North Australian Show, the Royal Windsor Horse Show, the British Horse Society, the South Saskatchewan Wildlife Association, the Northern Country Fair and Horse Show, the British Trust for Ornithology, the Canadian Cutting Horse Association and the Cumbria Wildlife Trust. The duke was associated with the World Wildlife Fund (WWF) for many years and was its first president from 1961 to 1982, international president from 1981 to 1996, and, on his retirement, he became president emeritus.

Since 2005, when she became a member of the royal family, the Duchess of Cornwall has accepted several invitations to become patron of animal charities including the Animal Care Trust. This organisation, part of the Royal Veterinary College, became a trust in 1982 when the late Queen Mother became its first royal patron. In May 2005, shortly after her marriage to the Prince of Wales, the Duchess of Cornwall agreed to become its patron and one of her first efforts was to help raise £5 million to develop the Queen Mother Hospital for Animals, which has now become the largest veterinary teaching hospital in Europe. Her Royal Highness is also patron of the Moorland Mousie Trust, which looks after the welfare of ponies on Exmoor; the British Equestrian Federation, which she joined in 2006 and in which she actively supports every form of equestrianism, especially in regard to the British Olympic team; and she is president of the Brooke Hospital for Animals. She is also patron of the Langford Trust, which is active in supporting the work of the University of Bristol's School of Veterinary Science, and the Lady Joseph Charitable Trust, which provides assistance to disabled competitors in para-equestrian dressage. The duchess has also become patron of the Marwari Horse Society, a body concerned with the welfare of this breed of horse, indigenous to Jodhpur, India.

The Prince of Wales is associated with over 400 organisations both civil and military, a number of which reflect his interest in animals and sport. Although he no longer plays polo, he remains patron of the Cambridge University Polo Club and attends their meetings whenever possible. Similarly, his active association with hunting ceased years ago, even before the ban on the sport, because of a back injury, but he retains an interest in hunting, though now, of necessity, it's 'drag' hunting, without the fox being the prey.

His Royal Highness's animal patronages and presidencies number nearly thirty, not including agricultural societies which are animal related. They include the Eriskay Pony Society, Send a Cow, the charity that helps thousands of families in Uganda, Kenya, Rwanda, Ethiopia, Cameroon, Zambia and Lesotho, the Aberdeen Angus Cattle Society, the Atlantic Salmon Trust (wild fishing is also another of his interests), the Australian Stock Horse Society, the Badger Face Welsh Mountain Sheep Society, the British Deer Society, the British Horse Loggers, the Clydesdale Horse Society, the Devon Cattle Breeders' Society, the Llandovery Sheep Festival, the Lleyn Sheep Society and the Marans Club – the traditional English Cuckoo Maran hens are renowned for their deep brown eggs and attractive cuckoo barred colouring. He is also patron of the

Mutton Renaissance Club, the North Country Cheviot Sheep Society, the Poultry Club of Great Britain, the Rare Breeds Survival Trust, the Red Squirrel Survival Trust and the Riggit Galloway Society – this little-known breed of pedigree cattle was in danger of dying out before a group of enthusiasts came to the rescue and formed the society in 2007, with the active support of the Prince of Wales, who has done a great deal of work to help rare breeds. His Royal Highness also supports the South Devon Herd Book Society, the Southern Seabird Solutions Trust, the Sussex Cattle Society, the Welsummer Breed Poultry Club, the Wildfowl and Wetlands Trust and WWF-UK.

The Princess Royal is acknowledged to be one of the hardest-working members of the royal family with nearly 300 organisations to her name. Among those concerned with the welfare of animals are: the Animal Health Trust (president), the Beef Shorthorn Cattle Society (patron), the British Equine Veterinary Association (patron), the Durrel Wildlife Conservation Trust (patron), the Gloucester Old Spot Pig Breeders Club (patron), Hearing Dogs for Deaf People (royal patron), the Icelandic Horse Society of

Great Britain (member), the International Sheep Dog Society (patron), the Medical Equestrian Association (president), the Moredun Foundation (patron) – this Scottish organisation conducts scientific research into animal diseases, the National Equine Forum (president), the Racehorse Owners' Association (honorary member), the Royal (Dick) School of Veterinary Studies (patron), the Scottish National Fat Stock Club (patron), the Shorthorn Society of the United Kingdom of Great Britain and Ireland (patron), the Suffolk Horse Society (patron and honorary member), the Australian Veterinary Association (patron), the Horse Trust (patron), the International Centre for Birds of Prey (patron) – this is the oldest bird of prey centre in the United Kingdom, and the New Zealand Conservation Trust (patron).

The Duke of Gloucester is a member of the Lilongwe Wildlife Centre, which develops and provides benefits to the wildlife of Malawi.

The Queen's cousin, Princess Alexandra, is patron of the Belted Galloway Cattle Society and she is also patron of the Jacob Sheep Society. One of Her Royal Highness's more unusual and far-flung animal charities is called the Safe Haven for Donkeys in the Holy Land, of which she is royal patron. As the charity's name implies, it exists to assist working donkeys (and also horses) in Israel and Palestine.

Nearer home, Princess Alexandra is patron of the British Goat Society and the People's Dispensary for Sick Animals (PDSA), which offers free treatment for pets whose owners cannot afford to pay.

The royal family has only one rule when it comes to accepting a role in a charity – animal or otherwise: they are not prepared to be mere figureheads, though naturally they cannot devote as much time as they might wish to any one organisation. They insist that they are kept fully informed of the work of their charities and societies, and if there are to be any major changes, their approval must be obtained.

Appendix 2

List of Pembrokeshire corgis originally owned by the Queen and registered with the Kennel Club since Her Majesty came to the throne. Several of the dogs have had new owners as they were given by the Queen as gifts.

All corgis registered under Her Majesty's name have the prefix 'Windsor' to their names, apart from those registered by the late Queen Mother, which had 'Rozavel' as a prefix.

The dates refer to when the animals were included in the Kennel Club Register, not necessarily the dates of birth or death.

1957   Rozavel Lucky Strike
1961   Rozavel Beat the Band, Rozavel Honey Bee
1967   Blackie
1971   Brush

1971   Geordie

1971   George

1971   Foxy

1971   Whiteheather

1973   Dusty, Penny

1979   Emblem, Jet, Spark, Fable, Myth

1981   Ajax, Apollo, Diamond

1984   Puck, Beau, Kelpie, Legend, Phantom

1985   Dash, Lark, Ranger, Gambol

1987   Daniel, Fay, Mint, Phoenix, Pundit

1990   New Registrations – Litter (432)
       Hero, Pharos, Phiz, Dagger, Dawn, Dime, Disco,
       Ebony

New Registration – Litter (391)

1993   Flora, Minnie, Quiz, Swift

New Registrations (151) Litter (32)

2003   Dipper, Jay, Linnet, Martin, Plover, Robin, Wren

New Registrations (156) Litter (38)

2003   Bramble, Cedar, Holly, Jasmine, Larch, Laurel,
       Rose, Willow

Appendix 3

List of retrievers (Labradors) originally owned by the Queen and registered with the Kennel Club since Her Majesty came to the throne. A number of the Labradors had new owners once they left the Sandringham kennels.

All the dogs (yellow and black Labradors) have 'Sandringham' prefixes to their names. The Princess Royal's dogs have 'Tinglestone' as a prefix.

1953 Topsy
1954 Slipper, Candy (owned by the Duke of Edinburgh)
1955 Mint
1956 Copper, Storm
1959 Rock
1960 Bow, Snare, Cloud, Dagger, Toffee, Frost, Bracken, Ranger, Santa
1961 Bronco, Fargo, Comet, Flame, Flare

1962   Pancho, Mask, Rusty

1964   Flicker, Dakota, Mask, Texas, Flake, Fog, Ice, Sixpence, Avon, Nevis, Juniper, Angel

1965   Bill, Blae, Muick, Bonk, Flint, Jan

1967   Bliss, Gav, Bunting, Dipper, Plover, Skua

1968   Barney, Boko, Berry, Arfa, Laura, Dunlin, Finch

1969   Abyss, Cave, Gannet, Flora, Islay, Solo, Claret, Gordon, Bray

1970   Jessie, Jumper, Anton, Curler, Huntsman, Jack, Court, Hollyberry, Maureen, Isa, Reef, Dawn

1970   Ash, Daisy, Brogue, Flipper

1971   Arbour, Bel, Gan, Dunrock, Hawk, Moss, Gelder, Micras, Boots, Clog, Dubbo, Skid, Garym Gairn, Mona

1973   Lantern, Tilly, Mercury, Pike, Pillow, Shadow, Shandy, Dee, Harvey, Stiletto

1974   Wilma, Nellie, Bill, Bow, Blackbird, Jackdaw, Cygnet, Dipper, Oscar, Sinbad, Tiber, Tickler, Quinn, Farquhar, Fergus

1975   Francis, Brent, Copper, Geordie, Ian, Moscar, Nighthawk, Smith, Dinah, Buaa, Christy

1976   Dart, Fleet, Vesper, Capper, Cloud

1977   Mandarin, Gem, Mustard, Hawkins, Jubilee

1978   Trip, Ginger, Adventure, Crystal, Dollar, Eskimo, Glimmer, Kestrel, Penguin, Marquis, Swinbrook

1979   Diamond, Gemma, General, Genial, Gleam,

Glitter, Needle, Pincer, Randal, Slip, Spike, Wicket, Clive, Clove, Fennel, Mint, Mustard, Parsley, Safron, Thyme, Bramble, Dakota, Douglas, Fargo, Flipper, Fury, Hermit, Mist, Mull, Reef, Ribbon, Tay, Test, Thames, Trent, Tweed, Tyne, Diego, Dirk, Ditty, Diver, Flake, Fog, Freeze, Tanya, Hawk, Toss

1980 Walrus, Kelpie, Khaki, Kindle, Kismet, Knell, Knot, Kris, Kukri, Mufti, Murmer, Muster, Bell, Derrick, Echo, Forties, Rig, Tug, Welder, Osprey, Eider, Salt, Tartar, Daring, Fortune, Gamble, Guide, Hazzard, Scout, Skittle, Venus, Virtue, Barry, Corona, Hydra, Jupiter, Mars, Phoenix, Virgo, Zenith, Whale

1981 Collar, Pintail, Primus, Crown, Gold, Kopje, Kraal, Trek, Anna, Dancer, Georgia, Natasha, Olga, Troika, Tsarina, Cape, Debbie, Dotterel, Downy, Durban, Hope, Kori, Tarquin, Kiwi

1982 Tui, Thistle, Buchan, Elf, Jet, Frost, Petrel, Shell, Tarmac, Tartan, Viking, Bluff, Cove, Curry, Dell, Dimple, Flint, Grit, Gulf, Gully, Hill, Lime, Mini, Pearl, Pebble, Pedlar, Penny, Ruby, Tarbuck, Tin-Tin

1984 Biretta, Bonnet, Bowler, Busby, Cap, Mitre, Stalker, Stetson, Trilby, Turban

1985 Kel, Marsh

1987   Dilys, Dolphin, Drama, Drummer Boy, Mick

1988   Alvis, Jaguar, Lagonda, Maxi, Minx, Rolls, Rover

1989   Monk

New Registration – Litter (6346)

1990   Bob, Bonny, Daring, Grace, Pieman, Star, Surf

New Registration – Litter (6900)

1991   Burn, Don, Esk, Gairn, Gelder, Sanquar, Slate, Squire, Streamer

New Registration – Litter (7905)

1993   Maestro, Metro, Royce

1993   Tinglestone Cutlass, Tinglestone Hussar, Tinglestone Rapier, Tinglestone Sword

New Registration – Litter (8187)

1994   Flow, Grant, Grenade, Gremlin, Jet-Setter, Kinn, Sandy, Spate

New Registration – Litter (8844)

1995   Guy, Thetis, Triton

New Registration – Litter (6805)

1996   Samantha, Sarah, Sherry, Shingle, Shona, Starlet, Steven

New Registration – Litter (7698)

1997   Boost, Dash, Spark, Spur Adam

New Registration – Litter (9946)

1998   Jaunty, Len, Pride, Swagger, Tam, Vanity, Beecham, Boult, Mariner, Mehta, Sargent, Wood

1999   Tinglestone Cedar, Tinglestone Corley, Tinglestone Larch, Tinglestone Maple, Tinglestone Willow

2003   Crofter, Guardsman, Hamlet, Moss, Ready, Rum, Rupert, Russet, Rustler

2005   Boris, Carlos, Carmen, Figaro, Lacey, Mimi, Salome, Siegfried, Toby, Tosca

2009   Cody, Flush, Guthrie, Jackson, Lottie, Muffin, Treacle

Appendix 4

List of English spaniels owned by the Queen and bred at Sandringham kennels; all have the word 'Sandringham' as a prefix to their names.

1978 Tweed

1979 Pear, Plum, Mango, Maxwell

1980 Fern, Holly, Ivy, Lichen

1981 Tern, Tramp, Sloe, Spot, Dusky

1987 Dagger, Kris, Kiwi

2008 Arch, Broom, Brush, Duster, Rough, Tidy

N.B. It is interesting to note that, as the Queen names all her dogs herself, she has displayed a remarkable sense of occasion and amusement at times. In 1984 she borrowed hat names for her Labradors; in 1988 it was British motor cars. And with the cocker spaniels, both in 1980 and 2008, there was a theme running through the naming process.

Select Bibliography

Among the books consulted are the following.

Blaikie, Thomas, *Corgi and Bess* (London: Fourth Estate, 2006)

Boothroyd, Basil, *Philip: An Informal Biography* (London: Longman, 1971)

Campbell, Judith, *The Queen Rides* (London: Lutterworth Press, 1965)

Cathcart, Helen, *The Queen Herself* (London: Star, 1983)

Clayton, Michael, *Prince Charles: Horseman* (London: Stanley Paul, 1987)

Crawford, Marion, *The Little Princesses* (London: Cassell, 1950)

Daly, MacDonald, *Royal Dogs* (London: W. H. Allen, 1952)

Gordon, Sophie, *Noble Hounds and Dear Companions* (London: Royal Collection, 2007)

Hoey, Brian, *Anne: The Private Princess Revealed* (London: Sidgwick & Jackson, 1997)

Hoey, Brian, *At Home with the Queen: The Inside Story of the Royal Household* (London: HarperCollins, 2002)

Hoey, Brian, *Her Majesty: 60 Regal Years* (London: Robson, 2012)

Hoey, Brian, *Zara Phillips* (London: Virgin, 2008)

Holden, Anthony, *Charles, Prince of Wales* (London: Weidenfeld & Nicolson, 1979)

Lister-Kaye, Charles, *Welsh Corgis* (London: W. & G. Foyle, 1971)

MacDonogh, Katharine, *Reigning Cats and Dogs: A History of Pets at Court since the Renaissance* (London: Fourth Estate, 1999)

Rose, Kenneth, *King George V* (London: Weidenfeld & Nicolson, 1983)

Rush, Len, *Captain of the Queen's Flight* (London: Bloomsbury, 1987)

Whitfield, June, *Dogs' Tales* (London: Robson, 1987)

About the Author

Brian Hoey has been a writer and broadcaster for over forty years and was one of BBC Television's first newscasters. He secured the first ever TV interview with the Queen's daughter, Princess Anne, and has subsequently covered many royal events over the years, including the weddings of Prince Charles and Lady Diana Spencer in 1981 and Prince Andrew and Sarah Ferguson in 1986. He was also a commentator at Princess Diana's funeral in 1997.

Hoey has written more than thirty-five books, many of them about the British royal family, including *Not in Front of the Corgis*. He is the official biographer of the Princess Royal, Princess Anne.